Out-of-Left-Field

Out-of-Left-Field

BASEBALL TRIVIA

ROBERT OBOJSKI & WAYNE STEWART

Main Street
A division of Sterling Publishing Co., Inc.
New York

Library of Congress Cataloging-in-Publication Data Available

2 4 6 8 10 9 7 5 3 1

Published by Sterling Publishing Co., Inc.
387 Park Avenue South, New York, NY 10016

This book is comprised of material from the following titles:
Baseball Bloopers & Other Curious Incidents © 1989 by Robert Obojski
Baseball's Strangest Moments © 1988 by Robert Obojski
Baseball Oddities ©1998 by Wayne Stewart

© 2006 by Sterling Publishing Co., Inc.

Distributed in Canada by Sterling Publishing
c/o Canadian Manda Group, 165 Dufferin Street,
Toronto, Ontario, Canada M6K 3H6
Distributed in the United Kingdom by GMC Distribution Services,
Castle Place, 166 High Street, Lewes, East Sussex, England BN7 1XU
Distributed in Australia by Capricorn Link (Australia) Pty. Ltd.
P.O. Box 704, Windsor, NSW 2756, Australia

Interior Design: Tilman Reizle/Oxygen Design

Sterling ISBN-13: 978-1-4027-4213-2
ISBN-10: 1-4027-4213-4

For information about custom editions, special sales, premium and
corporate purchases, please contact Sterling Special Sales
Department at 800-805-5489 or specialsales@sterlingpub.com

CONTENTS

BATTING

1

INSULTING CASEY

WHEN MICKEY MANTLE CAME UP with the New York Yankees at the beginning of the 1951 season, he was one of the most highly touted rookie ballplayers of the twentieth century.

Only nineteen, Mickey already had two years experience in professional ranks and had enjoyed a banner season in 1950 with Joplin, Missouri, of the Class C Western Association, hitting a league-leading .383 and knocking in 136 runs.

Mantle, a murderous switch-hitter labeled "can't miss," began the '51 campaign for the Yanks in good style at bat as he delivered key base hits and drove in his share of runs. Manager Casey Stengel, however, noted that Mantle's work at his rightfield position left something to be desired, so Stengel spent many hours personally coaching Mickey on the finer points of patrolling the outer pastures.

ONE DAY IN EARLY JUNE, Casey was showing Mickey how to field balls that caromed off the right-field barrier at Yankee Stadium. Stengel, wearing an outfielder's glove, set himself into playing position and said, "This is the way I used to play bounces that ricocheted off this barrier."

Mantle looked down at Casey, not believing that this wizened old man could have ever been a ballplayer and blurted: "Like hell you did!" Casey was silent. (Actually, Stengel had played rightfield in the new Yankee Stadium in the 1923 World Series with the New York Giants when they clashed with the Yankees.)

The very next day Casey sent Mickey down to the minors where he spent the next six weeks with the Kansas City Blues of the American Association before Stengel called him back up to New York.

Stengel said later of the incident, "When I show a player how to do something and he gets smart-alecky with me, back down to the bushes he goes...and I don't care who he is."

Mickey learned his lesson the hard way, and from that time on he made it a point to listen with respect to his manager.

DURING THE LATE 1950S when Mickey Mantle was at the peak of his career as a power-hitting Yankees outfielder, he made sports headlines when he signed his first contract calling for a six-figure amount, exactly $100,000. Just a generation ago, six-figure salaries for a full season's play were reserved for the really big diamond stars like Mantle, Joe DiMaggio, Stan Musial, and Ted Williams. Today, that kind of money won't even cover the salary of a third-string catcher.

In fact, each member of the 1988 Los Angeles Dodgers received nearly $109,000 as a winning share of the five-game World Series. And each member of the Oakland A's, who bowed to the Dodgers in the '88 Series, received a share amounting to just over $86,000. That's inflation for you!

TED WILLIAMS'S VISION

TED WILLIAMS, THE GREAT Boston Red Sox slugger (who averaged .344 over a nineteen-year big league career) was long noted for having particularly keen eyesight. One sportswriter went overboard when he claimed that Williams followed a pitch so closely that he could actually see the ball hit the bat.

In an interview Williams disagreed: "No one can ever see the ball hit the bat because it's physically impossible to focus your eyes that way. However, when I hit the ball especially hard, I could smell the leather start to burn as it struck the wooden bat!"

By mid-season 1946, Ted Williams was hitting nearly .400 and everyone in the American League was thinking of ways to throttle him. For starters, Lou Boudreau, Cleveland's crafty manager, introduced the "Williams Shift" where exactly six fielders were stationed to the right-field side of second base: first and second basemen and right-fielder, of course, and also shortstop, center-fielder and third baseman. It didn't help.

BIRDIE TEBBETTS, DETROIT'S CATCHER, thought he had a better idea. While crouching behind the plate one hot summer day at Briggs Stadium when Williams was at bat, Tebbetts let loose with a torrent of words as he began to relate a long and convoluted joke in order to break "the Splendid Splinter's" concentration.

Williams, who appeared to be listening intently, let the first pitch go by for a called strike. Then the second pitch flew by for another called strike.

Finally, Williams collected himself and slammed the third pitch for a homer deep into the second deck of the right-field stands more than four-hundred feet away.

After Williams loped around the bases and was about to touch home plate, he asked Tebetts, "What was the punch line to that joke?"

◆

BABE HERMAN'S BAT

BABE HERMAN REACHED his absolute peak as a hitter in 1929 and 1930, when he averaged .381 and .393, respectively, though he didn't win the league batting title in either year. Nevertheless, his .393 mark still ranks as the highest batting average in Dodgers history. In that fabulous 1930 season, Babe smacked out 241 hits, including forty-eight doubles and thirty-five homers, scored 143 runs, and drove in 135.

Herman "slipped" to .313 in 1931 and then was traded away to Cincinnati. Dodgers fans howled when the Babe was shipped out and many of them decided to boycott Ebbets Field games altogether.

After one year with Cincinnati, Herman was traded to the Chicago Cubs, then went to Pittsburgh, back to Cincinnati, and played a few games for Detroit in 1937 before he slid back down to the minors. In 1945, during World War II, the Babe came back to Brooklyn as a pinch hitter to close out his career.

IN 1,552 BIG LEAGUE GAMES played over thirteen seasons, Babe Herman averaged a solid .324. An average that high is usually good enough for Hall of Fame membership, but the Babe's questionable fielding has kept him out of the baseball shrine at Cooperstown.

The number of Babe Herman outfielding stories is endless. Tom Meany, a sportswriter who saw the Babe play many times, wrote in the old New York *World-Telegram* on several occasions that Herman was in danger of being hit on the head whenever he went after a fly ball. Babe protested to Meany and declared that if he ever was struck by a fly ball he would never show up at Ebbets Field again.

"How about getting hit on the shoulders and arms?" Meany challenged.

"Oh, no! Getting hit on the shoulders and arms don't count," Herman begged off.

Babe Herman did lead all National League outfielders in errors for three straight seasons, but for his entire major league career his fielding average came out to .971, and that isn't too shabby.

What if the Designated Hitter Rule has been instituted a half-century ago? Babe Herman would have stayed in the big leagues for at least twenty years—and his batting statistics would have been awesome.

◆

BO JACKSON STRIKES OUT

YOU KNEW THAT "BO" JACKSON was the 1985 Heisman Trophy winner from Auburn University. You knew that he broke all sorts of collegiate football records as a running back and that in 1987 he began a successful pro-grid career with the National Football League's Oakland Raiders. But did you know that in his first twenty at-bats for Auburn, Jackson not only failed to get a base hit, but struck out every time he came up? Nevertheless, professional baseball scouts felt that Jackson had all the necessary ability to become a diamond star. He proved them right by eventually becoming a reliable long-ball hitter for the Kansas City Royals.

◆

WILLIAMS AND RUTH

T ED WILLIAMS IN 1941 enjoyed a banner year as he swatted a fat .406 going 185 for 456—and that's the last time a major leaguer reached the .400 mark for a full season.

Williams put together the rare combination of hitting with power for average, as he rapped out seventy-three extra base hits (thirty-three doubles, three triples and thirty-seven homes). Pitchers feared "the Splendid Splinter," walking him 145 times, giving Williams a fantastic on-base percentage of better than .550.

More remarkably, Ted struck out only 27 times, and thus he established an all-time record of walking 118 times more than he fanned. In 1942, Williams again walked 145 times, though his strikeout total increased to fifty-one.

Before the great left-handed slugger was through, however, he put together four more seasons in which he walked one-hundred or more times than he fanned. Those seasons are: (walks given first) 1946—156, 44, plus 112; 1947—162, 47, plus 115; 1949—162, 48, plus 114; and 1954—136, 32, plus 104. In 1951, Ted just missed the 100 more walks than strikeouts standard when he went 143-45.

In his nineteen seasons in the majors (1939-60, with three years out for military service in World War II), Ted Williams walked 2,018 times (a figure second only to Babe Ruth's), and fanned on 709 occasions, giving him a "plus of 1,309 in that category, far and away a big league record.

BABE RUTH RECEIVED 2,056 free passes during his illustrious 22-year career (1914-35), and struck out 1,220 times, giving him an excellent "plus" of 726. Though the Babe's high mark of 1,330 K's stood as a record for a long time, Ruth never fanned one-hundred times in a single season.

Ruth reached his season high-water mark in strikeouts in 1923 when he fanned a league-leading ninety-three times, but he also walked 170 times, an all-time major league record. Some baseball historians estimate that at least eighty of those walks were intentional, but that figure is strictly unofficial.

Ruth's strikeouts were almost as dramatic as his home runs. He seldom waved at a pitch when he missed it…he always took a full strong cut, whether he missed the ball by a foot or drove it 450 to 500 feet for a homer.

The only other major leaguer to record one-hundred or more walks over his strikeout figure in a single season was Eddie Stanky of the Brooklyn Dodgers. In 1945 he went 148 and 42 for a "plus" 106.

Lou Gehrig came close in 1935 when he walked 132 times and took thirty-eight K's for a "plus" ninety-four.

◆

FUN WITH STATISTICS

IN THE PAST, PLAYERS who pounded out three-thousand or more base hits in their careers always wound up with lifetime batting averages well over .300. For example, Ty Cobb averaged .367 on 4,191 hits, Tris Speaker came in with a .344 mark on 3,515 hits, and Stan Musial finished at .331 on 3,630 base hits.

In recent years, however, the trend has been for players to reach the three-thousand-hit milestone and average less than .300. Al Kaline was the first to perform the "feat." After twenty-two years with the Detroit Tigers (1953-74), he collected 3,007 hits but averaged only .297.

Lou Brock became the second 3,000-hit-minus-.300 man.

Playing with the Chicago Cubs and St. Louis Cardinals from 1961 through 1979, Brock racked up 3,123 hits and averaged .293.

Carl Yastrzemski amassed 3,419 base hits (giving him seventh place on the all-time list) in his twenty-three-year career with the Boston Red Sox (1961-83). Since Yaz came to bat 11,988 times officially, however, his average came to a full fifteen points below .300, namely .285, and thus he went into the record books as the third three-thousand-hit-minus-.300 man.

Yastrzemski had his peak years during the American League's low average era. In 1968 he led the league in batting with a .301 mark and was the only A.L. player that year (with enough times at the plate to qualify for the hitting title) to reach .300.

OAKLAND IN 1968 led the league in batting with a puny .240 while the A.L. as a whole averaged a miserable .230. The New York Yankees brought up the year with a horrendous .214.

Robin Yount, the Milwaukee Brewers veteran center-fielder, stands the best chance of becoming baseball's fourth 3,000-hit-.300 man. Through 1988, Yount at thirty-three and with fifteen years in the majors behind him, had registered 2,407 base hits and a .290 average.

♦

SOME HALL-OF-FAMER

WHEN MICKEY MANTLE was elected to the Hall of Fame in 1974, he had the dubious distinction of becoming the first out-fielder-first baseman to enter baseball's shrine at Cooperstown, New York, with a lifetime batting average *below* .300. When he wound up his eighteen-year career with the New York Yankees in 1968, Mantle came in with a .298 batting mark, though he averaged .300 or better for ten seasons and twice topped .350.

However, Harmon Killebrew, the former Washington Senators-Minnesota Twins long-ball hitter, had the even more dubious distinction of being the first outfielder-first baseman named to the Hall of Fame (in 1984) to go through an entire career without ever having hit .300 in any full season. (In his debut year in the majors in 1954, Killebrew did manage to go four for thirteen, .308, in nine games.)

During his twenty-two years in the big leagues, Killebrew averaged only .256, the lowest of *any* Hall of Fame position player, but he more than made up for this by slamming 573 homers, the most by any American League right-handed slugger. Harmon "the Killer" Killebrew also knocked in 1,584 runs.

Yaz never had a two-hundred-hit season

Carl Yastrzemski has the distinction of being the only one of the fourteen major leaguers to achieve the three-thousand-hit plateau without having had a single 200-hit season. The closest Yaz came to the two-hundred-hit level was in 1962, his sophomore year, when he rapped out 191 safeties. He also led the A.L. in base hits in 1963 and 1967 with 183 and 189, respectively.

Yastrzemski holds the American League record for getting one-hundred or more hits in twenty-two seasons.

"YOU'VE GOT TO HAVE THE KILLER INSTINCT"—REGGIE JACKSON

"ANYONE WHO SAYS THE WORLD SERIES is 'just another game' is not a champion," declared Reggie Jackson during an interview in Oakland-Alameda County Coliseum when the Oakland Athletics and Los Angeles Dodgers were tangling in the '88 World Series. Jackson went on to say:

"The World Series is different and you must play the game different. You got to have that mental tenaciousness…you got to rise to the occasion…to put it bluntly, you've got to have the killer instinct to be a World Series hero."

Jackson, who became known as "Mr. October" for his exploits in post-season playoff and World Series competition, declared:

"I had nothing in mind in October but success. It's like Jim Brown used to say about football and like Paul Newman said in *Cool Hand Luke*, you got to get your mind right. You can't be nice in championship play…you've got to be more than a little mean, you've got to be very mean."

Apparently, Jackson knows whereof he speaks, for he slammed eighteen homers in post-season play, eight in playoffs and ten in the World Series. In one of the greatest individual performances in baseball history, Reggie, as a member of the New York Yankees, belted three homers against Los Angeles in this decisive Game 6 of the 1977 World Series. In that Series, Jackson hit a record total of fivehome runs, scored ten runs, drove in eight, and personally broke the backs of the Dodgers.

◆

JOE D'S STREAK

DID YOU KNOW THAT Joe DiMaggio's record of hitting safety in fifty-six consecutive games was beaten? By Joe himself? Yes, in 1933 he had a streak of hitting safety in sixty-one consecutive games when he was an eighteen-year-old rookie with the San Francisco Seals in the Pacific Coast League. He kept the streak going from May 28 through July 25 by pounding out 104 hits in 257 official at bats for a .405 average.

Joe DiMaggio in 1951 was nearing thirty-seven, not all that old, but the "Yankee Clipper" was obviously past his prime as he struggled to keep his batting average from going below the .260 mark.

Going into Cleveland's Municipal Stadium for a late July game against the very tough Cleveland Indians, Joe was still batting fourth, the "clean-up spot," but he wasn't driving in runs with his usual consistency.

Cleveland had big fireballing right-hander Mike "Big Bear" Garcia on the mound to tame the Yankees, who were in first place in the American League pennant race by a slim two-game margin over the Indians.

In the top of the seventh inning, with the score tied, 1-1, Garcia got into a bit of a jam as he had a runner on second base with one out. Yankee first baseman Joe Collins, batting third, came striding up to the plate and Garcia proceeded to take an action that hitherto was considered unthinkable. He was ordered by manager Al Lopez to walk Collins intentionally to get at DiMaggio. Mel Allen, broadcasting the game for the Yankees, muttered almost in disbelief, "I can't recall any pitcher intentionally walking the man preceding DiMaggio in the lineup."

Joe D himself probably winced a bit as he came to the plate. On Garcia's first deliver, however, he mistakenly threw a belt-high fastball; the Yankee Clipper connected and sent a vicious line drive that went whistling past Garcia's ear and out into center-field for a single, scoring the man from second. No one was going to show up the great DiMaggio—and that RBI single turned out to be the game winner for the Yankees.

NEVERTHELESS, DIMAGGIO KNEW the end was coming and other situations would probably follow where pitchers would similarly challenge him, and situations where the aging DiMaggio might fail to come through.

That '51 season ended successfully for the Yankees. They captured the pennant by a comfortable five games over the runner-up Indians and then whipped the New York Giants in the World Series four games to two.

DiMaggio wound up the regular season batting .263 (the lowest average of his career by far), drove in a respectable seventy-one runs in 116 games, but found that he was being "rested" more and more frequently by manager Casey Stengel. In the World Series, D batted in five key runs and played his center-field position flawlessly.

In December, the Yankees offered DiMaggio a second consecutive $100,000 contract for the 1952 campaign (big money in those days), but he demurred and said: "Sure, I'd like to play another year for a six-figure salary, but it wouldn't be DiMaggio out there." Thus ended the Yankee Clipper's active career.

As Rudolf Bing, the longtime Metropolitan Opera impresario, once said, "In any profession, it's better to quit too soon than too late."

◆

DUMPING A JAPANESE HERO

JAPAN'S BIGGEST BASEBALL STARS are generally rewarded with managers' posts at the conclusion of their active playing careers. And Sadaharu Oh, the great slugger who blasted 868 regular season homers in a twenty-two-year career with the Central League's Tokyo Giants (1959-80), was no exception to this custom.

After serving as a coach for three years, Oh, called "the Japanese Babe Ruth," was appointed manager of the Giants. And during a five-year stretch his team never won the "Japan Series" (an affair that pits the pennant winners of the Central and Pacific leagues in a best-of-seven playoff).

Oh's Giants captured one pennant in 1987, but lost the Japan Series to the Pacific League's Seibu Lions. After the Giants finished a "miserable" third in the six-team Central League in 1988, Oh was summarily fired, an act that sent shock waves throughout Japan. Oh's legion of fans thought be had a lifetime job as manager because of his towering hero status.

Once he was given the axe, Oh made these comments which are reminiscent of those made by U.S. big league managers when they are fired:

"Over the past five years I have not been able to meet expectations, and I accept that. In this world of professional sports, you have to win. That's the bottom line."

The Japanese are certainly beginning to sound as if they're being Americanized!

◆

DEPRESSED O'DOUL

FRANK "LEFTY" O'DOUL, a native of San Francisco, played in his first professional baseball game with Des Moines, Iowa, of the Western League in 1917 at the age of twenty.

O'Doul started out as a pitcher, receiving trials with the New York Yankees and Boston Red Sox, and then switched to the outfield because of arm problems. From 1924 through 1927 O'Doul ranked as one of the top hitters in the Pacific Coast League, with his best year of production coming for Salt Lake City in 1925 as he rapped out 309 base hits in 198 games, averaging a cool, .375.

After piling up 278 base hits in 189 games and averaging .378 for the San Francisco Seals in 1927, O'Doul was called up by the New York Giants for the following season. And so at the age of thirty-one Lefty O'Doul was finally in the big leagues to stay for a while.

For the next seven years he terrorized National League pitching, winning two batting crowns. He found himself in a Philadelphia Phillies uniform in 1929 and proceeded to lead the league with a .398 mark as he racked up 254 hits, still a National League record. While with Brooklyn in 1932, he paced N. L. hitters again, this time with a .368 mark.

And how was O'Doul rewarded by the Dodgers for winning a batting title? Was he given a substantial raise? Absolutely not! He was cut by $1,000, from $9,000 down to $8,000. Remember this was 1932—the midst of the Great Depression—and economy was the order of the day in regard to baseball salaries.

O'Doul concluded his big league playing career during a second tour of duty with the New York Giants in 1934 (he hit .316) and then began a long managerial career in the Coast League, starting with the San Francisco Seals in 1935.

Lefty O'Doul (he threw and batted left-handed) kept himself on the Seals active roster as a pitcher and occasional pinch hitter, and made his final appearance in a Seals game in 1945 as a substitute batter. Lefty was now forty-eight.

After O'Doul left the Seals following the 1951 season, he made P.C.L. managerial stops at San Diego, Oakland, Vancouver, and Seattle. While with Vancouver in 1956, Lefty inserted himself into a late season game as a pinch hitter and delivered by smashing a booming triple that hit the fence in right-center field. O'Doul refused to take himself out of the game in favor of a pinch runner and scored when one of his charges singled to center.

At the age of fifty-nine, Frank Joseph "Lefty" O'Doul had become the oldest man in the history of professional baseball to get a base hit in a regular season game.

WE SPOKE WITH O'DOUL about his history-making triple in the fall of 1959 at his San Francisco restaurant and bar. Lefty recalled: "The pitcher underestimated me. He apparently thought about my age at the time—nearly sixty—and he threw me a fairly easy pitch to hit and I really unloaded. Since I began playing as a pro in 1917, my first and last base hits came almost forty years apart. I don't believe any other player could make a statement like that."

Lefty O'Doul died in 1969, but he continues to be remembered as one of baseball's most colorful personalities and each year the drive to have him elected to baseball's Hall of Fame grows stronger. As a major league player, O'Doul batted a robust .349 in eleven seasons.

Moreover, he helped lay the groundwork for the creation of Japan's first professional baseball league—the Central League—in 1936. He even named Tokyo's entry in the Central League as the Tokyo "Giants" since he was playing for the New York Giants when the circuit was in the planning stages.

O'Doul visited the Orient many times, conducted numerous baseball clinics at Japanese colleges and universities, and played a major role in reactivating professional baseball in Japan immediately after the conclusion of World War II.

◆

BASEBALL'S STRONG MAN

JIM RICE, STANDING SIX FEET TWO INCHES tall and weighing 220 pounds, for years ranked as one of the physically strongest men in the major leagues. He slammed out numerous tape-measure homers for the Red Sox, some traveling distances of five-hundred feet. His best year was 1978, when he hit for the circuit forty-six times, and by the end of the 1988 season, Rice approached the four-hundred-homer mark.

His awesome strength became graphically apparent one day when Rice was standing in the batter's circle taking practice swings when suddenly his bat broke in half. He had gripped the war club so tightly and swung so hard that the wood simply splintered from the force of the practice swing.

Don Zimmer, Boston Red Sox manager at the time, who viewed the incident, said: "In over thirty-five years of baseball, I've never seen a player break a bat that way before. Only a man with Paul Bunyan strength could do it."

◆

TWO RECORDS IN ONE DAY

ON THE EVENING OF FRIDAY, August 19, 1988 at Detroit, Carlton Fisk, forty-year-old Chicago White Sox catcher, broke an American League record by appearing in his 1,807th game behind the plate. (Rick Ferrell had held the old record for catchers of 1,806 games.)

Fisk celebrated the occasion by going five-for-five, singling four times, tripling, and driving in two runs. This was Fisk's first five-hit game in his nineteen years in the majors. Despite Fisk's perform-ance the Tigers beat the White Sox that night 5-4.

"I didn't do anything differently in this game," Fisk told reporters later. "On other occasions, I've hit the ball hard four or five times and every drive went straight into an outfielder's glove. There are some things about baseball you just can't explain."

◆

COBB'S DAY

DURING A DETROIT TIGERS "Old-timers' Day" staged at Briggs Stadium in July 1951, a young reporter went up to Ty Cobb (a life-time .367 hitter and charter Hall of Fame member) and asked: "Mr. Cobb, what do you think you would hit if you were playing today?"

"Oh, about .300," answered Cobb.

"Is that all?" said the reporter incredulously.

Cobb countered without batting an eye: "Well, don't forget I'm sixty-five years old."

◆

THE GREAT BAMBINO

BABE RUTH LIKED TO LIVE LIFE to the fullest and often his appetite for pleasure and frolic proved to be his undoing. He became the world's best-known athlete not only for his prodigious home-run hitting, but also because of his outrageous antics on and off the field. The public's appetite for any bit of news about "the Sultan of Swat" was insatiable.

On one occasion, for example, after a night on the town in Manhattan, he hailed a cab. After he was deposited at his apartment door, the Babe reached into his pocked and handed the cabbie what he thought was a $10 bill.

"Keep the change!" boomed the generous Babe…the cab fare had come to only about $2.

The taxi driver's eyes almost popped out of his head as he glanced at the bill. With a lightning-quick motion he grabbed it and raced off with his hack.

Unfortunately, because his eyes were a bit glazed over, Ruth didn't realize until later that he had given the driver a $1,000 bill!

"I'd better look at my money a little more carefully before I spend it," the Babe said with a touch of remorse in his voice.

AS THE 1925 SEASON DAWNED, George Herman Ruth, then thirty, was at the height of his career. In his ten major league seasons he had succeeded in becoming the dominant force in the game.

In a game at Tampa toward the end of spring training, the Babe had slammed a couple of tape-measure homers. He then went on to celebrate by gorging himself on a yard or two of hot dogs and what amounted to nearly a bucket of soda pop.

This time the Bambino really overdid it. He became violently ill and was rushed to a New York hospital for an emergency stomach operation. Front-page headlines everywhere recorded Ruth's illness as a national crisis, with clergymen of all faiths holding special services calling for Ruth's recovery. The Babe came close to death, but as one of the surgeons on the case said, "Only his youth and strength saved him." This was known as "the bellyache heard 'round the world."

Ruth didn't get into the Yankees lineup until early June, missing the first six weeks of the season. And for the first two or three weeks, he had trouble keeping his average over .250, because he was still weak from the effects of the stomach operation.

The Babe's disposition suffered and this led to memorable clashes with Yankee manager Miller Huggins. Among other things, the two had a number of dugout shouting matches, but little "Hug," a veteran of twenty-five years in the majors as a player and manager (he stood five feet four inches and weighed 145 pounds soaking wet), backed down to no man, not even to the great Babe Ruth.

Matters came to a head toward mid-August on a long train trip home from St. Louis (where the Yanks had played the Browns) when Ruth tried to throw Huggins off the moving train. The Babe perpetrated this outrage half-jokingly, but Hug was not amused and slapped G.H.R. with a $5,000 fine, the most costly ever levied on a ballplayer to that date.

Ruth was absolutely livid and blustered into the office of Yankee owner Colonel Jacob Ruppert, threatening to quit if the fine wasn't rescinded, and Huggins fired. "The fine sticks and Huggins stays," Ruppert told him in no uncertain terms.

The Babe knew when he was licked, and from that point he acted like an all-American Boy Scout and finished the season with twenty-five homers and a .290 average, not bad at all considering his horrendous start at the beginning of the baseball season.

Nevertheless, Ruth's absence from so many games hurt the Yankees as they finished a dismal seventh in 1925, posting a losing 69-85 (.448) record.

The Bambino went all out in 1926 to redeem himself, enjoying a banner year as he paced the Bronx Bombers to a pennant, batting a robust .372 and leading the league with forty-seven homers and 145 RBIs. (Interestingly, the Yankees then proceeded to pile up thirty-nine consecutive winning seasons, a record string for any team in professional sports. It wasn't until 1965 that New York dropped below the .500 mark again.)

The Yankees clashed with the St. Louis Cardinals in the 1926 World Series, and after Huggins' charges whipped the Cards 2 games out of three in St. Louis to take an overall 3-2 lead, the New Yorkers were in a jovial mood on the one thousand-mile train ride back to the Big City. Ruth was in particularly high spirits and, after having several high-powered drinks long the way, he spotted Colonel Jake Ruppert by himself in the club car. Ruth went over and gave the Colonel a bear hug. By the time he was through mauling the Yankees' distinguished-looking owner he had succeeded in ripping the colonel's tailored shirt off his back.

Ruth and his teammates had a good laugh over this incident, but Ruppert was absolutely furious. Unfortunately, the Yankees dropped the next two games to the Cardinals and lost the World Series 4-3. Again, Jake Ruppert was not amused.

THERE IS ONE BABE RUTH TRAIN RIDE, however, that has not been as widely publicized as the Huggins and Ruppert incidents. This particular rail journey occurred in about 1930 during one of the post-season barnstorming trips down South that Ruth himself had organized with other major leaguers.

One late afternoon as the train chugged through a small town, the Babe spotted a group of teenage boys playing a pick-up baseball game in an open field. Since the train had to stop for water, Ruth jumped out of the train, walked over to the field, and got himself involved in the game.

In the process, he gave the boys tips on batting, fielding, throwing, and sliding. Ruth took off his suit jacket and demonstrated the techniques of sliding into a base as he kicked up a minor sandstorm in the process.

After thirty-five or forty minutes, with the train more than ready to proceed, the Babe dusted himself off and reluctantly got back into his car.

"Who was that man?" asked one of the boys.

"Why, that was Babe Ruth himself!" came the answer.

"I don't believe it," said another incredulously. He should have believed it, for this episode actually happened and was filmed by one of Ruth's teammates who had a movie camera with him. He recorded nearly the entire scene on film, a film that has been shown periodically on commercial television.

STORIES ABOUT BABE RUTH showing kindness to kids are prolific. The Babe was raised in an orphanage, experienced much unhappiness as a boy, and as an adult compensated for this barren spot in his early life by going out of his way to treat youngsters with a great deal of fatherly affection.

Babe Ruth achieved the rare combination of hitting for power and average. His best season for average came in 1923 when he finished at .393 while drilling forty-one homers and driving in 131 runs. Over his twenty-two-year career (1914-35), the Bambino averaged a healthy .342, a percentage good enough to give him ninth place on the all-time list of batters who came to the plate officially at least five thousand times.

Once, when discussing hitting with a reporter, the Bambino declared: "Hell, I coulda averaged .600, but all my hits would have been singles."

Babe Ruth established so many records that it requires several pages just to list them all, but one of his least-known records concerns his hitting accomplishments while he was a pitcher. The Babe is the only pitcher in big league history (with at least one-hundred games on the mound to his credit) to have hit .300 or better lifetime. In 163 games as a pitcher (mostly with the Boston Red Sox from 1914 through 1919), Ruth averaged .304. His batting prowess is what led to his sale to the Yankees in 1920.

Wes Ferrell, generally conceded to be the best hitting pitcher on a career basis, could manage only .280 average. In a fifteen-year career (1927-41), Ferrell also set a pair of home run records for a pitcher: most in one season, nine in 1931, and most in a career, thirty-eight.

◆

FOOT-IN-THE-BUCKET

"HE'LL NEVER BE A HITTER," chided the critics in 1924 as they watched Al Simmons, rookie Philadelphia Athletics outfielder, take batting practice in spring training.

The twenty-two-year-old Simmons had averaged better than .360 in three minor league seasons, but his unorthodox batting style bothered his managers and coaches.

Simmons, batting right-handed, is said to have kept one "foot-in-the-bucket" (an affliction common to sandlotters)—that is, he kept his forward foot (left foot) at a pronounced angle toward third base rather than forward, toward the pitcher. This stance, however, enabled Simmons to keep his front foot free so that he could hit to any field.

Simmons went on to hit .308 in his rookie year with the A's, and in his second season he collected 253 base hits (the most ever by a right-handed hitter) and averaged .384. When A's manager Connie Mack was asked what he thought of Simmons's "foot-in-the-bucket" stance, he replied: "I don't care if he stands on his head so long as he keeps murdering that ball!"

Simmons never changed his batting style through a twenty-year career in which he banged out 2,927 hits, averaged .334 and drove in 1,827 runs. He won back-to-back batting titles in 1930-31 when he averaged .381 and .390, respectively, as he paced the A's to American League pennants in both years.

Though Al Simmons may have looked like a rank sandlotter at the plate he was dreaded by every pitcher in the league. He gained election to baseball's Hall of Fame in 1953.

Hank Ruszkowski, a big right-handed-hitting catcher who had several trials with the Cleveland Indians from 1944 to 1947, had an even more peculiar batting stance than the one used by Al Simmons. Ruszkowski used to hold his bat with the barrel touching the ground as he waited for the pitch. While watching him in that stance in an exhibition game at Cleveland Stadium, we saw him hit a home run that carried at least 425 feet.

Batting stances can be a relative matter.

◆

STRANGE PINCH HITTER

IT WAS SUNDAY, AUGUST 19, 1951, at Sportsman's Park, St. Louis, as the last place Browns tangled with the Detroit Tigers, who were also deep in the second division. The game was meaningless as far as standings were concerned.

During the season Bill Veeck, flamboyant owner of the Browns, had become a bit desperate because his ragtag team floundered badly at the gate. (Total paid admissions for the year came to a sorry $294,000.)

As the late summer game progressed before the usual sparse Sportsman's Park crowd, Browns' manager Zack Taylor sent in a pinch hitter names Eddie Gaedel, who had never appeared in a professional game before. Tigers' right-hander Bob Cain walked Gaedel on four straight pitches, and after Eddie trotted down to first he was replaced by pinch runner Jim Delsing.

By this time the crowd was in an uproar. Pinch hitters had walked before, but none of them were as small as Gaedel, who stood three feet seven inches tall and weighed 65 pounds, the normal size for a genuine midget. As Gaedel, wearing the number 1/8 on the back of his uniform short, swung his seventeen-inch bat menacingly at pitcher Cain, he hollered, "Throw the ball right in here and I'll moider it!"

He had been told what to do. Bill Veeck wrote in his autobiography, "I spent many hours teaching him to stand straight up, hold his little bat high, and keep his feet sprawled in a fair approximation of Joe DiMaggio's classic style. I told him I'll kill him if he swings the bat."

Plate umpire Ed Hurley had questioned Gaedel's credentials as a player, but under Veeck's able direction the midget had produced a standard major league contract from his hip pocket.

Bill Veeck, the "Barnum of Baseball," in all his years in the game had never gone this far before and succeeded in pulling off the greatest single outrageous stunt in the history of the game.

On the next day American League President Will Harridge turned thumbs down on any future Tom Thumbs by outlawing any further such travesty of the game.

Bill Veeck may have gained an enormous amount of notoriety for sending a midget to the plate, but nothing he did could save his franchise. After the 1953 season he was forced to sell the Browns, who in 1954 were transformed into the Baltimore Orioles.

As for Eddie Gaedel, his place in the standard baseball record books is secure. He complied a perfect record as a pinch hitter, getting on base in his only time at bat.

◆

HIT A HOMER, WIN A SWORD

EARL AVERILL, CLEVELAND INDIANS hard-hitting center-fielder, was a part of the delegation of American League All-Stars who traveled to Asia in the fall of 1934 to play a series of sixteen-exhibition games against a team consisting of Japan's top amateur and semi-professional players called the "All-Nippon Stars."

Averill's teammates included stars Babe Ruth and Lou Gehrig, sluggers Bing Miller, Charlie Gehringer, and Jimmie Foxx, and pitchers Lefty Gomez and Earl Whitehill. The exhibitions were staged in cities throughout Japan, and by the time the series ended in late November the Americans had made a clean sweep by winning all sixteen games.

One particular game between the Japanese and the Americans played at Itatsu Stadium in Kokura, an industrial city on the island of Kyoshu, revealed quite graphically the almost limitless enthusiasm the Japanese have for baseball. Rain fell the night before the game, which was scheduled for 2 o'clock on November 26 and the precipitation continued steadily as game time approached. The fans, however, didn't allow bad weather to prevent them from seeing a contest they had been eagerly anticipating, particularly since this was the only appearance the two teams would make in Kokura.

Hard-core baseball aficionados began lining up at the gates outside the park at 5 in the morning and when the gates opened around noon some eleven thousand persons had "bleacher" tickets. The catch was that there were no seats in the bleachers, which consisted only of the bare outfield turf. Unfortunately, the outfield was by then ankle deep in water and the hardy bleacherites had to stand, kneel, or squat in the shallow lake for the entire game. (The total crowd reached twenty-thousand that day since Itatsu Stadium had nine-thousand permanent seats in addition to its "bleacher" capacity.) The fans in the outfield did not permit this minor inconvenience to dampen their enthusiasm for the big game, nor were they too disappointed when the All-Nippon Stars lost 8-1. They saw a well-played contest and for the first time got a chance to view up close the big American stars, Babe Ruth and Lou Gehrig, about whom they'd read and heard so much.

One spectator, a middle-aged shopkeeper, walked eighty miles to see the game at Kokura, and he carried a sword which he vowed to give to the first American smashing a home run against the All-Nippon Stars. This valuable trophy was won by Earl Averill who drove a long homer into the right-field seats. It was the highest possible honor he could have received: Among the Japanese, a sword was not only a weapon, but also the warrior's badge of honor—it was thought to be his very soul.

When we spoke with Averill at Cooperstown's Hotel Otesaga in July 1981, two years before his death, he recalled the 1934 Japanese tour and the game in Kokura: "That Japanese sword is the most unusual and prized trophy I ever received in baseball, and I've kept it in a glass case at my home in Snohomish [Washington] all these years."

Averill hit eight home runs on the 1934 exhibition series, while Babe Ruth paced the long ball parade with thirteen homers. The trip to Japan marked Babe Ruth's last appearance in a New York Yankees uniform, incidentally, since in February 1935 he was handed his unconditional release.

◆

GET THE X-RAY MACHINES READY!

IN A MID-AUGUST 1987 game against the San Francisco Giants, New York Mets third baseman Howard Johnson poled a mighty home run at Shea Stadium that allegedly measured about 480 feet. Roger Craig, Giants manager, charged out of the dugout and told the umpires the bat should be impounded and turned over to league officials for examination.

"There's no way Howard Johnson could hit a ball that far without the bat being corked," Craig fumed.

The Johnson bat was taken the National League president A. Bartlett Giammati's office and from that point it was sent out to a nearby hospital where it was X-rayed for cork. The X-rays proved negative. No cork was found in the barrel.

According to newly established major league rules, the manager of each team is allowed to challenge one bat during the course of a game. Since challenges are being registered in so many games, both the National and American League offices are considering buying their own X-ray machines in order to cut down on fees being paid to hospitals!

When cork is placed in the barrel of a bat, the batter is able to speed up his swing and hit for greater distances. Bats are supposed to be constructed of wood and no other substance.

When manager Craig registered his protest, he noted Howard Johnson never hit more than twelve homers in one season in his big league career through 1986 and he slammed more than thirty-six in 1987. He believed equipment tampering caused this phenomenon.

Ah, but Craig didn't realize that Johnson has been on well-planned weight and strength programs and had no need for corked bats in order to sock baseballs into orbit.

◆

HIT ON HEAD BY BAT WHILE
IN ON-DECK CIRCLE

IN 1945, MOBILE CATCHER HARRY CHOZEN had hit safely in thirty-three consecutive games and was on his way to setting a new Southern Association record of hitting safely in forty-nine consecutive games. Then, while kneeling in the on-deck circle, he was hit on the head and knocked unconscious by a flying bat that slipped out of the hands of teammate Pete Thomassie as he followed through on a vicious swing. Chozen was forced to retire from the game. After this episode, Chozen proceeded to hit safely in sixteen additional games before being stopped. Southern Association President Billy Evans was called upon to rule and decided that Chozen's failure to get a hit in that July 6 game where he had walked in his only time at bat before being knocked out, did not break the hitting streak. The record Chozen broke had stood for twenty years.

Chozen's record is interesting in several other ways. Twice during the streak he was used as a pinch hitter and delivered. On two other occasions he entered the game in late innings, batting only once in each game, but he still managed to get his base hit. He broke the previous record of forty-six in a truly dramatic manner by smashing a long home run in his first time at bat in his forty-seventh game. (Chozen's only big league experience came in 1937 at the age of twenty-two, when he caught one game for the Cincinnati Reds. He had a single in four trips to the plate.)

IN AN AUGUST 1978 GAME, Los Angeles Dodgers catcher Steve Yeager wasn't quite as lucky as Harry Chozen in a batting circle accident. A Dodgers hitter broke his bat on a pitch causing a jagged piece of ash to sail straight for Yeager's throat. The team's trainer and doctor worked with lightning speed to remove the splintered wood from the jugular vein area. Yeager might otherwise have choked and bled to death. After a couple of weeks on the disabled list, Steve was back in action.

◆

"INKY"

ALAN "INKY" STRANGE, American League shortstop of the 1930s and early 1940s was a brilliant fielder wherever he played and a strong minor league hitter who could never quite solve major league pitching.

Strange came up with the St. Louis Browns in 1934 at the age of twenty-four, played 127 games, and hit a weak .233 when higher averages were in vogue. He started the 1935 campaign with the Browns, found himself traded to Washington in mid-season, and then spent the next four years in the minors.

He had his "career year" in pro ball in 1939 with Seattle of the Pacific Coast League when he clubbed a circuit-leading fifty-five doubles while performing with his usual aplomb in the field.

That earned him a promotion back to the St. Louis Browns in 1940 where he remained through 1942, being used primarily as a utility infielder. After that, Strange never again resurfaced in the majors. In a total of 314 American League games, he hit .223.

Why couldn't a player of Strange's considerable ability ever quite make it in the big leagues? It seems that he couldn't hit a good curve ball. Once pitchers discover a player is primarily a fast-ball hitter, they feed him a steady diet of curves. That's what happened to Strange.

Baseball historian Bill Borst, who has written several books and numerous articles on the St. Louis Browns, observed: "Alan Strange typified the average Brownie…he had a great deal of promise but that promise was never really fulfilled.

◆

"NOT NOWHERE"

YOGI BERRA IS ONE OF THE POWER HITTERS of yesteryear who almost always seemed to get his bat on the ball, and managed to keep his strikeouts down to an extremely low level.

When he came up with the Yankees at the tail end of the 1946 season, Berra indicated quite clearly through his performance in the seven games he got in that he wasn't going to let too many third strikes slip by him. In those seven games he bashed two homers and struck out only once. From that point on, Berra, a lefthanded pull hitter who was built like a fireplug (he stood five-feet-eight-inches-high and weighed a solid 190 pounds), enjoyed five full seasons where his homers exceeded his K's: 1950—28, 12; 1951—27, 20; 1952—30, 24; 1955—27, 20; and 1956—30, 29.

In nearly two decades of big league play (1946-65), covering 2,120 games, Yogi hit 358 homers against only 415 strikeouts. Moreover, in fourteen World Series from 1947 to 1963, covering seventy-five games, Berra hammered twelve homers against only seventeen strikeouts.

Berra didn't play at all in 1964 when he managed the pennant-winning Yankees, and, after he was fired for losing the World Series, he landed on his feet as a coach for the New York Mets in 1965.

The struggling Mets needed an extra catcher badly, and so, Berra, then forty, was pressed into service. Berra saw action in only four games before he threw in the towel. In one of the games he struck out three times and told reporters afterward: "I never struck out three times in one game before: not in the big leagues, not in the minor leagues, not in the little leagues, not nowhere. Now it's time to quit for good."

If everyone in the big leagues today who struck out three times in one game would voluntarily retire himself, the playing ranks would be almost decimated.

◆

FLAMINGO STYLE

SADAHARU OH, THE FAMOUS Tokyo giants left-handed-hitting first baseman, early in his career adopted an unusual batting style. He kicked up his right leg in flamingo style and then planted his left foot on the ground at the moment of contact of bat and ball. Some of his critics said he looked like "a one-legged swinging scarecrow," but in a twenty-two-year career that stretched from 1959 to 1980 Mr. Oh managed to belt 868 regular season homers, far and away a world professional record.

Hank Aaron, the U.S. major league home run champion hit "only" 755 homers. The Japanese insist that their two six-team professional leagues, the Central and the Pacific, are true major leagues. (The Tokyo Giants play in the Central League.)

Most American baseball experts agree that Oh easily could have succeeded in the U.S. big leagues, though he wouldn't have hit as many homers, since the Japanese ball parks are a bit smaller than those in the States.

Oh, born on May 20, 1940 in Tokyo, the son of a Japanese mother and a Chinese father, stood five feet ten inches and weighed 180 pounds in his playing days. Though he never broke Roger Maris's single season record of sixty-one homers in a 162-game season, he did reach fifty-five in his best season in 1964 in the Japanese league regular season of only 140 games.

Called "the Japanese Babe Ruth," Oh was appointed as Tokyo Giants manger, after his retirement from active play.

◆

TIGER ON THE BASE PATHS

"TY COBB IS ABSOLUTELY the greatest ballplayer I've ever seen on the diamond, and that includes everyone I've either played with or against," declared Joe Sewell, Hall of Fame infielder, in an interview conducted in the summer of 1987 at Cooperstown's Hotel Otesaga.

Sewell went on to say:

"When not in uniform, Ty Cobb personified the true Southern gentleman, but once he put on the Detroit flannels, he seemed to change character, almost like a Jekyll and Hyde. He played every inning of every game as if it were the critical point of a World Series…Even when he took his position in the outfield, he appeared like a tiger ready to spring.

"When he came roaring into second base on a close play, or to break up a double play, he reminded me of a runaway locomotive. He loudly proclaimed that the base line belonged to him and felt justified in running over any infielder who got in his way. But anyone who saw me play knows I didn't bail out when Cobb barreled into second base. I gave him as much as he gave me."

No question about that because Sewell, who stood only five feet seven inches and weighed 160 pounds, had the reputation of being a very scrappy and aggressive shortstop (later in his career he switched over to third base). He made up for his lack of size with his own special brand of ferocity.

In continuing to recall Ty Cobb's exploits on the baseball diamond, Sewell said:

"When I played again Cobb in the 1920s, he was getting well on into his thirties, but age didn't stop him a bit from being a demon on the base paths. Remember that Cobb was never the fastest runner in baseball, not even when he came up to the Tigers as a kid in 1905. But he knew how to run because he studied how to stride properly…he learned to cut yards off the distance between bases by knowing how to make sharp turns and how to tag the bag on the inside. He ran in straight lines. How many times do you see players today making wide turns and running any number of unnecessary yards in circling the bases?

"Sure, I pick Ty Cobb as the greatest ballplayer of all time, even ahead of Babe Ruth," Joe Sewell pontificated without a noticeable trace of doubt in his voice. "Remember that I played against Ruth during his peak years…and I was his teammate on the Yankees in the early 1930s when he was still going good. Ruth hit all those home runs, but Cobb could whack the ball as hard as anyone. I know firsthand because I caught lots of his drives that nearly broke my hand.

"The sportswriters began getting on Cobb in the mid-1920s because he was still content to hit singles and doubles when the home run was just coming into vogue. So he decided to show everyone he could match Ruth or anyone else for power. If I remember correctly, it was at St. Louis' Sportsman's Park in early May 1925 that Cobb decided to take a full swing and put on a real power exhibition. In the first game of the series, he went six for six and clubbed three homers, and on the next he hammered two more homers—that was five in two days and enough to tie the major league record. As I recall he got two doubles in those two games that nearly cleared the wall. He just missed seven homers in two days.

"Then Cobb went back to his natural snap swing batting style, but he proved his point that hitting home runs was no great trick."

◆

A TOUGH BATTER TO STRIKE OUT

JOE SEWELL BROKE INTO the big leagues under both tragic and dramatic circumstances. He was called up by the Cleveland Indians from the New Orleans Pelicans of the Southern Association on August 18, 1920, the day after their regular short-stop, Ray Chapman, was killed by a pitch thrown by the New York Yankees submarine artist Carl Mays at the Polo Grounds, New York. Chapman is the only player in major league history to have been killed during the course of a game.

Sewell stepped right into the shortstop slot and, with his timely hitting and good fielding, helped the Indians capture both the American League pennant and a World Series victory over the Brooklyn Dodgers.

Sewell remained with the Indians through 1930, playing mostly at shortstop, and then spent the final three years of his career with the New York Yankees as a third baseman. In fourteen years of big league action, Sewell, a left-handed hitter, banged out 2,226 base hits in 1,903 games and had a batting average of .312, a sound enough record to earn him Hall of Fame election in 1977.

Amazingly enough, Sewell struck out only 114 times in those 14 years, in over eight-thousand total plate appearances (including walks, sacrifices, etc.). He whiffed but three times in both 1930 and 1932, and he struck out only four times in three other seasons— and all these where when he was a regular playing in well over one-hundred games per year.

Joe Sewell is the all-time big league champion in being the toughest man to strike out.

When we spoke with Sewell in July 1987 in Cooperstown, we asked him why so many of today's hitters are fanning so frequently, pointing out that some of them roll up 114 strikeouts even before the season winds into August.

"Because they don't keep their eye on the ball!" snapped the eighty-nine-year-old Sewell, who is still very much alert, sharp-tongued and sharp-minded. "Too many batters today swing wildly trying for the home run instead of just going with the pitch and meeting the ball. If you're talking about strange baseball, it's strange to me why so many contemporary players lack discipline and refuse to control their swings the way they should."

Sewell added:

"Don't forget that the pitchers I faced in the 1920s and 1930s were just as fast as the ones throwing today. I faced flame throwers like Walter Johnson and Lefty Grove and they had a hard time striking me out because I had a compact swing and watched the ball the whole way. It's hard for me to imagine that legions of batters in the 1980s are striking out 125 to 150 times and more per season and not getting farmed out."

That may be because they have multi-million-dollar contracts.

JOE SEWELL WAS AN AUTHENTIC "IRON MAN" of his day, playing in 1,103 consecutive games from 1922 to 1928. At that time Sewell's Iron Man performance ranked second only to that of Everett Scott, American League infielder who played in 1,307 games in a row from 1916 to 1925. Sewell's streak ranked as No. 5 on the all-time list. Lou Gehrig stood No. 1, of course, with his staggering total of 2,130 straight games.

When asked why his streak came to a halt at 1,103, Sewell replied: "One morning I got up and found out I had the flu real bad and so I had to crawl right back into bed. Still, no one made a big fuss about playing streaks fifty to sixty years ago. At that time my 1,103 straight games plus a dime would be good for a cup of coffee."

(Cal Ripkin, Jr., Baltimore Orioles shortstop, established a big league record by playing 8,243 consecutive innings over the course of 908 games, but was pulled out in the eighth inning on a September 14, 1987 game by his father, manager Cal Ripkin, Sr., who said: "I wanted to get everybody to stop writing about the consecutive inning streak. The media pressure on us was getting intense, and so we just had to put an end to the streak.")

Sewell also recalled this interesting bit of history: "Lifetime records didn't attract all that much attention in the old days. I remember when Tris Speaker, our manager and center-fielder at Cleveland, got base hit No. 3,000 in 1925…there was hardly a ripple about it. the newspapers made passing mention of this milestone, but 'Spoke' received nothing in the way of special tributes."

Clifford Kachline, former Hall of Fame historian and longtime baseball writer, commended that Ty Cobb received relatively little publicity when he lined out base hit No. 4,000 while playing for the Philadelphia A's in 1927.

"Just check Cobb's file in the Hall of Fame Library and you won't see any banner headlines about that milestone," Kachline said.

Also there's no record of the President in 1927 calling from the Oval Office in the White House to congratulate Cobb. When Pete Rose broke Stan Musial's National League base hit record of 3,630, Ronald Reagan got right on the White House phone to call Rose before Pete had a chance to take his post-game shower. And when Rose got hit No. 4,192 in 1985 to pass Ty Cobb on the all-time list, Mr. Reagan got on the White House phone again to congratulate Pete.

"Everybody is statistics-happy today, even the President of the United States," muttered Joe Sewell.

◆

THE THREE-YEAR-OLD SLUGGER

PETE ROSE'S FATHER HARRY was anxious to get his firstborn son started in baseball at the earliest possible age, so little Pete began at just two years to catch thrown balls. When Pete was three he started out as a slugger. The first time he remembers slugging, he connected solidly with a pitch served up by his dad, and drove a hard rubber-coated ball to right-center-field, over and out of the backyard ball field and against a glass windowpane that promptly cracked in the kitchen of the Rose home on Braddock Avenue in Cincinnati.

That long drive by the Cincinnati Red, who holds baseball's all-time career record of 4,256 hits, was swatted on a summer Saturday in 1944. The crack is still in the window. According to a July 7, 1987, *New York Times* report, LaVerne Noeth, Pete's mother, was standing in the kitchen that day more than four decades ago when she heard the glass crack.

"My husband said, 'Hon, come here, look where Pete hit the ball,'" Mrs. Noeth recalled recently. "He said, 'I don't want it fixed. I'm going to show people where he hit that ball.' Pete was so small then, he was always small."

LITTLE HAS CHANGED IN THE NEIGHBORHOOD. Braddock Avenue is still a clump of homes on a hill above the Ohio River, five miles west of downtown, and boys still play ball there. At the old Rose household, members of Pete's family have no trouble finding first base in the backyard although the ball field is now covered with honeysuckle shrubs and black locust tress.

But the cracked window may soon disappear: the house is for sale. If anyone repairs that window, a slice of Americana will be lost.

After he hit that storied backyard liner at the age of three, Pete Rose continued playing ball at a furious pace, and he became so involved in various sandlot leagues that it took him five years to get through high school in Cincinnati. By having to spend that extra year, Pete didn't start his pro career with Geneva, N.Y. of the New York-Penn League until he was nineteen in 1960, when others began at eighteen.

If he had started in the minors a year earlier, he might have had an additional season in the big leagues and broken even more records. Pete didn't fail in high school because he was a bad student, mind you. His IQ had been measured as high as 150.

BEATING THE ENTIRE AMERICAN LEAGUE

HOME RUN HITTING CLEARLY REACHED ITS PEAK in the major leagues in 1987, as a record number of players (twenty-seven) hit for the circuit thirty or more times. Although there are so many sluggers going for homers, still there is no single slugger who dominates the long ball game as Babe Ruth did during the 1920s.

Ruth, in fact, on two separate occasions, in 1920 and 1927, personally hit more homers than each of the seven other teams in the American league. In 1920, "the Sultan of Swat" smacked out a record fifty-four homers and no team in the league matched that total. St. Louis came the closest with fifty, followed by Philadelphia with forty-four; Chicago, thirty-seven; Washington, thirty-six; Cleveland, thirty-five; Detroit, thirty; and Boston, twenty-two.

In 1927, the Bambino reached the peak of his long ball power as he whacked a record sixty homers, and that year no single A.L. team managed to top that total. Philadelphia "threatened" Ruth with fifty-six four baggers, followed by St. Louis with fifty-five; Detroit, fifty-one; Chicago, thirty-five; Washington, twenty-nine; Boston, twenty-eight; and Cleveland, twenty-six.

Most veteran baseball observers believe that no one could hit a baseball harder or farther than Babe Ruth when he was at his peak with the New York Yankees from 1920 to the early 1930s. Ruth's longest homer may well have been a six-hundred-foot shot he belted in a spring exhibition game at Tampa in 1925.

No one ever measured the velocity of his drives, but pitcher Mel Harder who came up with the Cleveland Indians in 1928 recalled the days when the Bambino batted against him at Cleveland's old League Park. This vintage-style ball park (now torn down) had a concrete wall topped by a wire fence running from right-field to right-center-field. "Ruth's drives often hit that concrete right-field wall with such tremendous force that the ball would bounce all the way back to second base," harder said. "Those balls would usually have to be thrown out of the game because they came back a bit flattened and carried a spot of green paint from the wall," he added.

◆

JIMMIE FOXX AND MICKEY MANTLE

IF JIMMIE FOXX HAD STUCK MORE closely to training rules, he could have piled up even more impressive statistics, for through the 1940 season, when he was only thirty-three, he had already smashed out an even 500 homers. From that point on, he was only able to hit thirty-four more in the big leagues.

Foxx stood an even six feet in height, weighed about 210 pounds, and was proportioned like a Charles Atlas with a massive chest and powerful forearms. Called "the Beast" because of his enormous strength (he developed his physique as a Maryland farm boy), he could hit homers right-handed as far as Babe Ruth could hit them left-handed.

As a member of the Boston Red Sox in 1938, he lined a shot to the deepest corner of the left-field bleachers at Cleveland's Municipal Stadium 435 feet away. Lots of hitters can blast baseballs 435 feet, but Foxx's line drive had so much velocity behind it that it broke the back of a wooden seat at that great distance!

On one occasion in batting practice Foxx hit a drive back to the box with such force that the pitcher could not get his glove up in time to shield himself (as Mark Eichhorn was able to do), and suffered a fractured skull. This particular pitcher, a promising youngster, saw his career ended on that fateful day.

Billy Martin once said Mickey Mantle could hit a baseball harder than anyone he ever saw…that may be true, but Martin never saw Ruth and Foxx in action. In deference to Mantle, however, his greatest moment of glory in the power department came on May 30, 1955, at Griffith Stadium when he faced Washington's Pedro Ramos.

Mantle, a switch-hitter batting left-handed, caught hold of one of Ramos' fastballs and propelled an immensely high drive that appeared to have enough power behind it to clear the rightfield roof, a feat that no player had accomplished in the stadium's half-century history. None of the great sluggers of baseball had even come close to powering a fair ball over the giant-sized filigree, the ornamental work hanging from the lip of the stands, which, in both right-field and left-field, hooks into fair territory toward the bleachers. Mantle hit the filigree, and as Joe Reichler, Associated Press baseball writer who witnessed the drive, said: "He came so close to making history that he still made it. The ball struck high on the façade, barely a foot or two below the edge of the roof…. For years after that spring 1955 game, fans who came to Griffith Stadium lifted their eyes and stared at the spot where the ball hit. Likely many of them remembered the fifty-six-foot homer Mantle hit in Washington two years before. Unobstructed, the drive against Ramos would have traveled even further."

◆

ONE TOUGH HOMBRE TO STRIKE OUT

MOST BASEBALL EXPERTS FEEL that the greatest single achievement in baseball was Joe DiMaggio's hitting in fifty-six straight games in 1941. Some say Joe D's most remarkable accomplishment was striking out only 369 times in his major league career in approximately eight-thousand total times at bat (including walks, sac flies, hit by pitcher, etc.)

Amazingly enough, Joltin' Joe hit 361 homers in his thirteen years with the New York Yankees (1936—51, with three years out for World War II military service), a figure only eight fewer than his total strikeouts! In his rookie year, DiMag fanned on thirty-nine occasions, and he never again struck out that many times in a season.

From that point on, DiMaggio enjoyed six seasons in which he had more homers than K's. Here are the fantastic figures, with homers first and strikeouts second: 1937—46, 37; 1938—32, 21; 1939—30, 20; 1940—31, 30; 1941—30, 13; 1946—25, 24; and 1948—39, 30. "The Yankee Clipper" almost made it again in 1950 when he slammed thirty-two homers against thirty-three strikeouts.

Even Bob Feller, baseball's unrivaled strikeout king from the mid-1930s through the 1940s, had a tough time fanning DiMaggio. Joe D, who had a career batting average of better than .320 against Feller, told us recently:

"Feller is best known for his great fastball, of course, but he also had a wicked curve which made him extremely effective. At the same time, he was a proud man and never tried too many curves against me…He almost always tried to blow the fastball by me—and since I pretty much knew what to expect I never had too much trouble with him."

We should emphasize here that DiMaggio never struck out much against anybody because he had extremely quick reflexes, perfect coordination, and keen eyesight.

◆

OH, JOE D

WHEN JOE DIMAGGIO, New York Yankees center-fielder, won the American League batting champion with a .381 average in 1939, he became the last right-handed hitter in the major leagues to hit .380 or better. Joe played in only 120 games in 1939 because he held out for more than a month at the beginning of the season. He finally settled for a contract calling for $30,000, a small fraction of what he could earn if he were playing today. All baseball salary comparisons are strange.

◆

"NEVER SWING CRAZY"

THREE TIMES IN HIS CAREER Johnny Mize posted records where his homers topped the totals of his whiffs. While with the New York Giants in 1947, the big left-handed-hitting first baseman bashed a career high fifty-one homers and fanned only forty-two times— and in the following year he hit for the circuit forty times against only thirty-seven strikeouts.

In 1950, as a member of the New York Yankees, Mize homered twenty-five times against twenty-four strikeouts. Overall, in a fifteen-year big league career (1936-53, with three years out for World War II military service, Mize rang up 359 homers against 524 strikeouts, an excellent ratio.

"I never swung crazy," Mize told us recently. "If the pitch was out of the strike zone, I just didn't go for it...I always tried to wait for my pitch," he disclosed.

Ted Williams, who possessed extraordinary vision, and who

knew how to control a bat as well as anyone in baseball, had four seasons in which his homers outnumbered his strikeouts. In this listing the homers are given first: 1941—37, 27; 1950—28, 21; 1953—13, 10; and 1958—28, 24. Overall, in a nineteen-year career (1939-60, with three years out for World War II military service), Williams hit 524 homers as opposed to 709 strikeouts, a superb ratio.

◆

BILL DICKEY

BILL DICKEY, THE HALL OF FAME New York Yankees catcher, is another throwback to an earlier era when some of the game's top power hitters were hard to fan. Though he didn't hit as many homers as DiMaggio, Mize, or Williams, Dickey still managed to have five seasons when his homers exceeded his strikeouts, and once when they were even (1933—14 and 14).

Those five sterling Dickey seasons are (homers first): 1932—15, 13; 1935—14, 11; 1936—22, 16; 1937—29, 22; and 1938—27, 22. In 17 seasons with the Yankees (1928-46, with two years out for World War II military service), Bill Dickey rapped out 202 homers against only 289 strikeouts.

Said Dickey recently: "In many ways baseball today is strange to me because so many big-leaguers—or supposed big-leaguers—are lunging at the ball in trying to get distance—and they're striking out three, four and even five times a game in the process."

◆

"SHOELESS" JOE

WHILE WITH THE CHICAGO WHITE SOX in 1920, Joe Jackson accomplished a feat that would be virtually impossible for a modern player to match—he actually had more triples than strikeouts, twenty to fourteen. While with the Cleveland Indians in 1912, "Shoeless" Joe lined out twenty-six triples, but we don't know if his three-baggers outnumbered his whiffs because strikeout records were not kept until 1913.

Compared to Joe Jackson, Dale Mitchell, who was active from 1946 to 1956, was a "modern" player in the strict sense. In any event, Mitchell was the last major leaguer, according to our best calculations, to triple more times than strike out in a single season. While with the Cleveland Indians in 1949, Mitchell, lefthanded slap hitter, tripled twenty-three times against only 11 strikeouts, a better than 2-1 ratio. Fantastic!

Sam Crawford, the all-time triples leader with 312, had one season we know about where his three-baggers exceeded his strikeouts: 1916—13, 10. ("Wahoo Sam" was with the Detroit Tigers at the time). Crawford may have had other triples-over-whiffs seasons, but Crawford's strikeout totals while he was with Cincinnati and Detroit from 1899 through 1912 were not kept.

Ty Cobb may have had at least one triples-over-whiffs season, but his 1907-1912 strikeout figures also are shrouded in mystery.

◆

HITTING WITH EXTRA OOMPH

DON MATTINGLY HAS BEEN NOTED primarily for his fielding and his high batting average. He smashed hard line drives to every part of the field, with homes runs merely a secondary affair until 1987. In his first four seasons with the New York Yankees (1983-86) Mattingly, a five-foot-eleven-inch 185-pound left-handed swinger, belted a good, not great, ninety-three homers, while batting the lofty average of .332.

In 1987, Mattingly continued his usual high batting average and modest home run-hitting pace. But, while hitting thirty homers, Mattingly, extraordinarily enough, was able to both tie and break two all-time major league home run records.

In July, he hit for the circuit in eight consecutive games, tying the major league mark established by Pittsburgh's Dale Long in 1956. Then on September 29 at Yankee Stadium against Boston he whacked his sixth grand slammer of the season, breaking the record of five that had been shared by Ernie Banks of the Chicago Cubs (1955) and Jim Gentile of the Baltimore Orioles (1961). Oddly, Mattingly had never hit a grand slammer before the 1987 season.

Mattingly's record-breaking sixth grandslammer came in the third inning off Boston lefthander Bruce Hurst. The ball carried eleven rows into the third tier of the right-field stands and powered the Yankees to a 6-0 victory over the Red Sox.

Mattingly had never hit Hurst well in the past, averaging a mere .217 with no homers.

When questioned by reporters after the game about his grand slam homer splurge, Mattingly modestly replied, "I can't explain it. I basically haven't done anything different other than to try to hit the ball hard. Before, I would hit a sacrifice fly with the bases loaded. Now, I think of hitting the ball hard. Consequently, if I get the ball in the air, it carries."

◆

KING OF THE WHIFFERS

AS FAR AS STRIKEOUTS are concerned, Bobby Bonds of the San Francisco Giants established the single season record in 1970 when he whiffed 189 times. Despite that horrendous whiff total, Bonds still managed to bat .302 and score 134 runs.

Bonds's whiff record may not stand up much longer, however, under the "onslaught" of today's free-swinging power hitters. Bo Jackson, for one, was well on his way toward a two-hundred-plus strikeout season with the Kansas City Royals in 1987, when he was benched for a long period, which happens when you don't get hits.

Babe Ruth for years held the all-time career strikeout record of 1,330, but in recent years many players have surpassed that figure. By the time Reggie Jackson, the all-time leading whiffer, retired after the 1987 season, he nearly doubled Ruth's total with more than 2,600 strikeouts.

◆

LIKE ROCKETS

BROOKS ROBINSON, the Baltimore Orioles Hall of Fame third baseman, said at an All-Star Game several years ago in response to our question: "I can't recall my strangest moment in baseball but I remember the scariest."

"One summer afternoon in 1969 or 1970, we were playing the Washington Senators at Baltimore and big Frank Howard, who was at his peak, sent a vicious liner that whistled just a few inches over my head. I didn't even have time to react to that drive, and within a split second I heard the ball strike the base of the bleacher wall some 370 feet away! If the ball had hit me full force, I might well have been decapitated. From that point on I played Howard deep, really deep…and I knew he would never call my bluff and bunt for a base hit."

Some time after the Robinson interview, we got hold of Frank Howard, a six-foot-seven-inch 265-pound giant of a man who likes like an overloaded truck, and asked him if any of his drives every knocked down an infielder. (Howard batted right-handed.)

"Not that I recall," answered Howard, one of baseball's most amiable men and now a Milwaukee Brewers coach, "but I did notice that almost all third basemen played me in the outfield grass."

BROOKS ROBINSON IS NOT UNUSUAL in being scared of line drives. Players who have been injured by jetlike drives have reason to be fearful.

Mark Eichhorn, the top Toronto Blue Jays' right-handed relief pitcher, working on the mound in the eighth inning of a Saturday afternoon, September 19 game (in New York's Yankee Stadium) threw a fastball to Yankees' outfielder Claudell Washington, who drilled a scorching line drive right back at Eichhorn.

Eichhorn instinctively moved his glove up to his lower chest in self-protection and luckily caught the ball. It was hit so hard that his left gloved hand was driven smack into his body and he was very nearly toppled over backward, but he still managed to hang onto the spheroid.

The Blue Jays trainer rushed out of the dugout to examine Eichhorn to see if there were any broken ribs or other injuries, but the big six-foot-three-inch 210-pound pitcher said he was okay and just needed a couple of minutes to pull himself back together again.

IF A PITCHER DOESN'T REACT quickly enough, a direct hit from a wicked line drive can cause serious injury, as would be expected. For example, Cleveland's ace left-hander Herb Score, in May 1957, sustained a severe eye injury when struck by a bullet line drive from new York Yankee shortstop Gill McDougal's bat. Mr. Score was washed up for the season and failed in several subsequent comeback attempts to regain his old form.

In the 1937 All-Star Game played at Washington's Griffith Stadium, St. Louis Cardinal ace Dizzy Dean tried to log a fastball past Cleveland's Earl Averill. A good fastball hitter, Averill rifled a savage liner back to the box. The ball struck Dean on the left foot and bounded away. Dean chased it down and nipped Averill at first on a close play, but when he reached the clubhouse he discovered his big toe was broken.

The play proved to be the turning point in Dean's career. He began pitching again long before the injury healed completely, and in doing so he was forced to change his motion. That placed an unnatural strain on his right arm and shoulder and he lost his great speed.

Dean hung on in the majors for several more years, but his glory days were over as he had to rely on guile rather than speed in trying to retire batters.

TALKING OF PLAYERS of an earlier era who could hit baseballs like rockets, Fred Lindstrom, the New York Giants star third baseman-outfielder of the 1920 and 1930s and a Hall of Famer, told us, at a 1978 Shea Stadium old-timers's game:

"When Rogers Hornsby was winning all those batting championships with the St. Louis Cardinals in the 1920s, he could hit a ball harder than anyone I saw. He batted right-handed, as you know, and all the infielders, including the second baseman, played him back on the grass…and many times I saw a Hornsby drive almost literally tear a fielder's glove off his hand. Lot of times, for example, the third baseman was just able to knock down a Hornsby shot, but the official scorers usually ruled a base hit because the ball was just 'too hot to handle.'"

◆

HOW FAST DO LINE DRIVES TRAVEL?

THE TOP SPEED MEASURED for any ball thrown by a pitcher is 100.9 miles per hour (Nolan Ryan, 1974), while a batted ball of the Claudell Washington line-drive variety under discussion here travels at least 150 miles per hour!

If a line drive travels 150 miles an hour through the pitcher's box, the Frank Howard liner over third base that scared Brooks Robinson could well have traveled 140 miles an hour plus.

◆

BRINGING ON THE DH RULE

AL BENTON IS BEST KNOWN in baseball trivia circles as the only major league pitcher to have faced both Babe Ruth (1934) and Mickey Mantle (1952) in regular season games, but he should be better known for his poor hitting. Benton, a big six-foot-four-inch 220-pound right-hander, broke into the big leagues with the Philadelphia Athletics in 1934 at the age of twenty-three.

In compiling a 7-9 season record, Benton faced the Yankees and Babe Ruth several times during the course of the 1934 campaign, Ruth's final year in the American League. (Ruth did play in twenty-eight games for the National League's Boston Braves in 1935 before retiring.)

Benton played the 1935 season with the Athletics, and then spent the next two years in the minors before reemerging in the majors with the Detroit Tigers in 1938. He remained with the Tigers through 1948, with a break while he served in the U.S. military during the height of World War II in 1943-44.

He saw action on the mound for the Cleveland Indians in 1949-50 and was shipped down to the minors for all of 1951, but the intrepid Benton came up with the Boston Red Sox in 1952 for his final year in the big leagues as a relief specialist, compiling a 4-3 record in twenty-four games. It was in 1952 that the forty-one-year-old Benton faced Mickey Mantle, then the new home run phenom, who had established himself as a star in his sophomore year with the New York Yankees.

Benton was a good journeyman pitcher, going 98-88 lifetime, together with posting a respectable 3.66 ERA, but his hitting was what should not be forgotten. It was moundsmen like Benton who helped make the Designated Hitter Rule an eventual reality in the major leagues, or at least in the American League. He was a shining example of pitchers who were such ludicrous hitters that they actually spoiled the look of the game.

Remember that Al Benton was a big man, as big and powerful a potential home run hitter as Hank Greenberg and Mark McGwire, but he stood at the plate like a wooden Indian, and usually took nothing more than halfhearted swings at pitched balls.

In his fourteen-year big league career, Benton batted 512 times, and managed to "eke out" fifty base hits for a horrendous .098 average. He hit exactly seven doubles, no triples and no homers (for a .111 "slugging" average), scored twenty-two runs, and batted in fourteen. He walked only 7 times, but struck out an even two-hundred times - truly an astonishingly bad batting record.

And for all those sad batting stats, Benton was not even baseball's poorest hitting pitcher—a few others (including Bob Buhl) had even worse records, strangely enough.

In all fairness, however, we cannot blame the pitchers entirely for this sordid state of affairs, since managers often told them, especially on hot, humid days, just to walk up to the plate, take three strikes, and sit down as quickly as possible so as not to waste energy running the bases.

AN ILLEGAL HITTER

THERE WERE MUTTERINGS for a DH rule as far back as the 1930s. Hitting was the dominant factor in baseball in the 1930s and eight batters out of nine got the job done, so the DH idea failed to take hold. Then much later, pitchers began to rule the game and scores were low, so the pitcher's turn at bat became more important.

Interestingly, several informal and abortive attempts at using a DH were made many years before the rule was officially adopted by the American League in 1973. For example, a little-known exception was made in 1939 when Chicago White Sox pitcher Bill "Bullfrog" Dietrich found himself struggling during the course of a hot midsummer afternoon against the Cleveland Indians at Comiskey Park, Chicago. Sox manager Jimmy Dykes went over to Cleveland manager Oscar Vitt and asked him if it was all right with Vitt if Dykes used a pinch hitter for Dietrich but allowed Bullfrog to remain in the game. "It's okay with me if it's okay with the umpires," said the gentlemanly Vitt.

The pinch hitter was used and Dietrich remained in the game!

◆

ZERO FOR SEVENTY

IN RESPECT TO ALL-TIME weak-hitting pitchers, Bob Buhl rates a top spot in that category. While with the Chicago Cubs and Milwaukee Braves in 1962, Buhl "distinguished" himself by going 0 for 70, winding up with a batting average of .000. No other player in major league history, pitcher or otherwise, has gone to bat that many times in a season without a single bingle.

Buhl struck out about half the time; 36 K's were registered against him during that ignominious 0 for 70 streak at bat, though he did manage to walk six times, and score two runs.

Over the course of fifteen years in the big leagues (1953—67), Buhl went 76 for 857, good for an .089 average, and somehow he managed two doubles which brought his "slugging" average up to .091. He scored a grant total of thirty-one runs, drove in twenty-six and struck out 389 times.

As a pitcher, however, Buhl posted a very competent 166-132 for a .557 percentage, reaching his peak in 1957 for Milwaukee when he went 18-7 as he played a key role in helping the Braves capture the National League pennant. Bob Buhl's record as a batsman literally cried out for the DH rule.

◆

RELIEF BATTERS

BATTING RECORDS FOR RELIEF PITCHERS are also quite awful. Hank Aguirre, a six-foot-four-inch 210-pound left-hander, who spent the majority of his career as a reliever, is renowned in baseball history for being an unusually weak hitter—and he had plenty of time to roll up a horrendous batting record since his pitching skills kept him in the majors for sixteen years (1955-70).

In 447 games, Aguirre came to the plate 388 times and managed to get exactly thirty-three hits, good for an .085 average. He rapped out seven doubles and one triple, giving him a .108 "slugging" average, scored fourteen runs and drove in twenty-one. He struck out 237 times, or about 60 percent of the time he came to bat.

Though Aguirre threw left-handed, he batted right-handed for the first decade of his major league career, and then in 1965 he decided to become a switch-hitter—but his average still remained in the lower depths.

Aguirre's lifetime pitching log is something not to be sneezed at as he posted a 75-72 won-lost record with thirty-three saves and a low ERA of 3.24.

WES STOCK was a highly reliable righthanded relief pitcher for the Baltimore Orioles and Kansas City Athletics in the American League for nine years (1959-67), as he won twenty-seven, lost thirteen, saved twenty-two, and fashioned a 3.60 ERA.

Stock's hitting was something else. A big six-foot-two-inch 195-pounder, he waved a very weak stick as he banged out exactly three singles in fifty-nine times at bat, good for an .051 batting average. Since he had no extra-base hits, the "slugging" average also came out to a cool .051. Stock had trouble making contact as he struck out thirty-seven times, or approximately two out of every three at-bats.

BOB FELLER may have been one of the greatest pitchers of all time, but as a hitter he adopted a batting stance so unusual that he looked like a pretzel twisted out of shape. Miraculously, he still managed to bat .151 lifetime.

We recall a big league game we saw at Boston's Fenway Park in the mid-1950s when a small boy of eight or nine asked his father: "Daddy, why does that man bat so funny?"

"Well," came the answer, "he's not supposed to be much of a batter, son, he's the pitcher."

EVEN KIDS ARE APPALLED at pitchers in the National League flailing away in the batter's box struggling to get base hits. Kids often can do better.

Vernon "Lefty" Gomez, the great New York Yankees moundsman, was such a terrible hitter that he joked about it constantly. When he had a triple bypass heart operation in the mid-1970s, Gomez remarked to a reporter: "That's the first triple I've had in my life." Gomez spoke the truth because in 904 major league at-bats, he had 133 base hits, including eleven doubles, but no triples or homers, which amounted to a .147 average (.159 "slugging").

Ironically enough, Gomez drove in the first run in All-Star history with a timely base hit. In the bottom of the second inning of the inaugural game played at Chicago's Comiskey Park on July 6, 1933, Gomez, facing "Wild Bill" Hallahan, lined a hard single to center-field scoring Jimmy Dykes from second base.

"That's why baseball is so interesting...the unexpected can happen anytime," said Gomez recently.

◆

YAZ

CARL YASTRZEMSKI STARRED for the Boston Red Sox for twenty-three years, and in 1983, at the age of forty-four, he became the oldest player in modern big league history to play regularly. Though "Yaz" was an outfielder for most of his career he saw service mostly as a designated hitter in 1983—his final season—as he played in 119 games, collected 101 base hits and batted a respectable .266.

In sporting the Red Sox uniform for nearly a quarter-century, Yastrzemski set an American League record by playing in the most games—3,308—and registering the most times at bat—11,988—while slamming out 3,419 base hits, good for a solid .285 lifetime batting average. He also won three batting championships (including a "Triple Crown" in 1967 when he swatted .326, bashed 44 homers and drove in 121 runs). He also tied a major league record by playing in one-hundred or more games for twenty-two seasons, and led the American League in intentional walks—190.

Carl Yastrzemski's endurance records were subsequently tied and/or broken by Pete Rose of the Cincinnati Reds. In 1985, the forty-four-year-old Rose, by then the Reds manager, played in 119 games (mostly at first base), tying Yaz, and in 1986, at the age of forty-five, he played semi-regularly (seventy-two games) at first before he benched himself permanently (as it turned out) in mid-August.

♦

HAPPY ANNIVERSARY!

LOU GEHRIG SWATTED his first career home run on September 27, 1923. On that same day fifteen years later, he hit his final blast. That truly is an incredible coincidence.

Likewise, on September 13, 1965, Willie "the Say-Hey Kid" Mays hit his five-hundreth home run. Exactly six years later, fellow longball artist Frank Robinson launched his five-hundreth.

Meanwhile, Eddie Mathews pelted his five-hundreth home run

on July 14, 1967. The next year on that day, long-time teammate Hank Aaron reached the 500 home-run plateau. By the way, these two men hit more four baggers than any other teammate duo— even more than Babe Ruth and Lou Gehrig.

◆

COMING AND GOING

ON SEPTEMBER 30, 1927, Babe Ruth propelled his sixtieth home run to set a single-season record. In that same contest, 531-game winner Walter "The Big Train" Johnson, like Ruth a charter member of the Hall of Fame, appeared in his final big-league game.

It should be noted that Johnson's last bow was not as a pitcher, but as a pinch hitter. Further, as a nice touch, Johnson flied out to Ruth to end his twenty-one-year stint in the majors.

◆

A SENSE OF COMPLETION

WHEN IT COMES to a sense of completion, consider what happened with Frank Howard back in 1968. Over a torrid stretch of twenty at-bats, the Washington Senators giant (six feet, seveninches and 255 pounds) smashed 10 home runs. He began his hitting binge versus Detroit's Mickey Lolich. He concluded the spree when he launched his 10th shot over the left-field roof of Tiger Stadium, a Herculean blow, against Lolich, of all people.

PITCHING

2

BILL BUCKNER'S BLOOPER

BOSTON WON THE FIRST TWO GAMES of the 1986 World Series against the New York Mets, lost the next two, won Game five and, in Game 6 at Shea Stadium, it appeared that the Red Sox would finally take their first world title since 1918.

The Bosox broke a 3-3 tie in the top of the tenth inning when they rallied twice. Dave Henderson led off the inning with a homer and then Wade Boggs drove in the second run with a double.

In the bottom of the tenth, reliever Calvin Schiraldi retired the first two batters, Wally Backman and Keith Hernandez, on fly balls, Boston was now within one out of winning the World Series—but Gary Carter kept the Mets' faint hopes alive when he singled. Pinch hitter Kevin Mitchell singled, and Ray Knight, with an 0-2 count, looped a single to center, scoring Carter as Mitchell advanced to third. Bob Stanley took over for Schiraldi at this point to hold off the surging Mets.

Mookie Wilson, the first batter to face Stanley, kept fouling off pitches as he worked the count to 2-2. Stanley's seventh pitch to Wilson was wild, and Mitchell raced home to tie the score, with Knight advancing to second base. With the count now at 302, Wilson fouled off two more pitches, and, finally, on Stanley's tenth delivery, Wilson slapped a hard grounder straight to Bill Buckner at first that looked like an easy inning-ending out. Somehow the ball got through Buckner's legs, and Knight raced home on the error giving the Mets a surprising 6-5 win that deadlocked the Series.

The Mets, with their lives so fortuitously extended, won Game 7 by an 8-5 count and became World Champions for the first time since 1969.

The Red Sox had come so close, but by now the dyed-in-the-wool Boston fans had become hardened to such agonies.

Boston manager John McNamara was severely criticized by Boston fans and sportswriters for not inserting a defensive replacement for Buckner in the late innings. For several years Buckner had been bothered by sore ankles that hampered his mobility in the field a bit. In order to protect his ankles he had become the only player in the major leagues to wear high-top spiked shoes.

McNamara's reply to his critics was: "Look, Billy Buckner played a key role in getting us into the World Series. He knocked in over one-hundred runs during the regular season, and—bad ankles and all—he was still an asset in the field...I had no thought of removing him from the game."

Buckner had, in fact, set a major league record for assists by a first baseman in a season with 184 in 1985, and in Boston's 1986 pennant year he led all A.L. initial sackers in assists with 157. In midseason 1987, Buckner was shipped off to the California angles.

Unfortunately, it appears that Billy Buckner will be mostly remembered for his blooper in Game 6 of the '86 World Series. Even the most talented of players can goof up in the clutch.

◆

SOUTHPAW

TENS OF THOUSAND OF major league ballgames have been played since 1876, with no two of them alike—and as the old axiom goes, "Anytime you go to the park there's always a chance of seeing something completely different."

Tommy John, forty-five-year-old southpaw pitcher for the New York Yankees, in his twenty-fifth season in the majors, made that axiom burst into life in a July 27, 1988 game at Yankee Stadium against the Milwaukee Brewers! Normally a good fielding pitcher,

Tommy committed three errors on one play, en route to a 16-3 win for his 285th lifetime victory.

In the fourth inning, John (1) bobbled Jeffrey Leonard's slow roller to the first-base side of the mound, (2) made a wild throw past first baseman Don Mattingly, and then, as Jim Gantner, who was on base ahead of Leonard, rounded third and headed for home, John (3) cut off right-fielder Dave Winfield's throw to the plate and made another wild throw—over catcher Joel Skinner's head and into the back wall.

Gantner would have been nailed by Winfield's throw, and Leonard would not have scored, but for John's three errors. Tommy thus became the first pitcher in modern major league history (since 1900) to achieve that dubious feat. The only previous pitcher with a triple error to his "credit" was Cy Seymour of the National League's New York Giants on May 21, 1898.

John jokingly told reporters after the game: "When I fielded the ball one-handed, I threw it like I was putting the shot...I should have eaten it. But with a thunderstorm coming through, there were a lot of negative ions in the air and, wearing a metal cup, it just glitched my mind."

TOMMY JOHN COULD afford to be funny, as he'd been laughing at Father Time for more than a dozen years. His career was supposed to be over in 1974 when he underwent a rare tendon transplant in his left elbow. After that, he won well over one-hundred games

Other pitchers have undergone similar tendon transplant surgery, a procedure now generally referred to as "the Tommy John Operation." His blooper in 1988 may well have shortened his long career.

HE JUST DIDN'T WATCH

BOB FELLER OF THE CLEVELAND INDIANS held the New York Yankees scoreless through the first eight innings in a 0-0 pitchers' battle in a July 1940 game at Cleveland's League Park. Red Ruffing was on the mound for the Yanks.

Then in the top of the eighth inning with two out and Red Rolfe on third base, Feller faced the great Joe DiMaggio. His first two pitches were wide and catcher Rollie Hemsley fired the ball back to Feller—a catcher's way of saying "Get the ball over the plate!" Rapid Robert's mind must have wandered temporarily for he didn't see the ball coming back at him until the last split-second, but by that time it was too late. Feller made a wild stab at the ball, and just managed to flick it with the webbing of his glove as it sailed out into center-field. Rolfe, on the alert, raced in and scored easily from second base. Feller was charged with an error, and the game ended 1-0.

When else has a pitcher missed a routine throw from the catcher, and allowed the winning run to score?

◆

THE KILLER INSTINCT

EARLY WYNN, who won exactly three-hundred games over a twenty-three-year major league career, was noted for his actual hatred of any player who came up to home plate to face him with a bat in his hands.

"Who was the toughest hitter you ever faced?" a reporter once asked Wynn.

"Well, there were two guys," replied Wynn. "One was named

Hillerich and the other was Bradsby."

(Hillerich & Bradsby is, of course, the well-known baseball bat manufacturing company based in Louisville, Kentucky.)

◆

A CURIOUS CASE

RUSSELL "BUZZ" ARLETT, a hulking six-foot-three-inch 225-pound mass of muscle reigned as one of the Pacific Coast League's biggest stars during the twelve-year period between 1919-30 as he sparkled on the pitcher's mound, at-bat, and in the outfield for the Oakland Oaks. As a right-handed hurler with an excellent curve and fastball, he topped the twenty-victory mark in each of three seasons and then, from 1923 on, he was consigned almost primarily to outfield duty because of his potent bat.

A switch-hitter, he averaged well over .300 regularly, topped the one-hundred RBI mark for eight straight years (1923-30), and in 1929, his banner year, he batted a fat .374, slammed thirty-nine homers and knocked in 189 runs. After hitting .361 in 1930 and stroking out 270 base hits in exactly 200 games, Arlett, now thirty-two, was finally given his first shot in the majors as the Philadelphia Phillies purchased his contract from the Oaks.

So how did Arlett do in 1931 for the Phils? Why, in 121 games he batted a potent .313 and piled up fifty-one extra base hits (twenty-six doubles, seven triples and eighteen homers), good for a hefty slugging average of .538.

Nowadays an outfielder turning in that kind of stat line would be screaming for (and getting) a three-year million-dollar contract. But how did Arlett do in his contract negotiations? It wouldn't be too harsh to say poorly. . .very poorly. He was sent back to the minors and never played another game in the major leagues!

While with the Baltimore Orioles of the International League in 1932, Arlett was still at the peak of his powers as he averaged .339, and led the league with fifty-four homers and 144 RBIs. In that '32 campaign, Arlett hit four homers against Reading on June 1 at Reading, and then in a July 4 game, he hit another four homers against Reading at Baltimore. No other player in professional baseball history has bashed four homers in a game twice in the same season.

Arlett continued to play into 1937, finishing his career with the Syracuse Chiefs of the I.L. Recently the Society for American Baseball Research (SABR) chose Buzz Arlett as the Greatest Minor Leaguer of all time. In 2,390 games, he picked up 2,726 base hits, averaged .341, ripped 1,037 extra base hits (598 doubles, 107 triples and 432 homers), scored 1,610 times, and drove in 1,786 runs (this does not include his year with the Phils).

As a pitcher with Oakland, he went 108—93 and compiled an excellent 3.45 ERA in a heavy-hitting era.

Why Arlett did not stick with the Philadelphia Phillies beyond a single season is a question that still mystifies baseball historians. Certainly his outfielding wasn't all that bad since in 1931 he committed only ten errors and had fourteen assists, a good number for an outer gardener. But as the old axiom goes, "There are certain things about baseball that cannot be explained."

◆

"HOW CAN YOU TELL DIZZY HOW TO PITCH?"

JAY HANNA ("DIZZY") DEAN, son of a poor Arkansas sharecropper, burst upon the big league scene in 1932 with the St. Louis

Cardinals and the big, brash right-handed fireballer averaged twenty-four victories a season over each of his first five campaigns.

Dizzy enjoyed his best season in 1934 when he posted a glittering 30-7 record to help lead the Cards to a National league pennant. Dizzy's younger brother Paul ("Daffy"), also a hard-throwing righthander, contributed nineteen victories to the pennant drive—thus, the two Dean boys won just over half of St. Louis' ninety-five victories.

Most good pitchers receive instruction from coaches for long periods and painstakingly develop techniques to make them effective moundsmen. Dean, a natural athlete, however, was entirely self-taught. Dizzy, who stood six feet three inches tall and weighed about two-hundred pounds, possessed a pitching style that was marked by a graceful and powerful rhythm; with a majestic sweep of his arm, he let the ball fly and kept poised and alert after the pitch. Throwing a baseball never held any mysteries for him and he believed wholeheartedly—without a shadow of a doubt—that he was the greatest pitcher in the world.

On one occasion a reporter came up to Dean and asked him how he came to be a great pitcher. Diz, whose tongue was often as sharp as his fastball, replied without a moment's hesitation: "I learnt everythin' myself....I jest like to rear back and fog 'em through!"

He relied on his great fastball to intimidate batters, and went on to lead the league I strikeouts for four straight seasons (1932-35). He set a modern national league mark for strikeouts in a single game when he fanned seventeen Chicago Cubs on July 30, 1944—a record that was later broken by Sandy Koufax, Steve Carlton, and Tom Seaver.

Dean, who maintained an absolute self-confidence as to his abilities (many players labeled him as an outright braggart), hardly concerned himself with listening to scouting reports about oppos-ing batters. "I never bothered about what those guys could hit or couldn't hit," he once chuckled. "All I knowed is they weren't gonna get a holt of that ball Ol' Diz was throwin'."

BEFORE A GAME AGAINST BOSTON early in the 1934 season, Dizzy loudly proclaimed to everyone within hearing distance that he wasn't going to throw a curve during the entire nine innings. He would unleash only his fastball. He didn't bend a curve all afternoon as he shut out the Braves 3-0, allowing only three sin-gles.

Dean often drove his catchers batty by insisting on pitching to a hitter's strength. He never worried about playing it safe. "A great pitcher is supposed to strike 'em all out the hard way," Dizzy rea-soned, and that's what he always tried to do, at least during the peak of his career.

Frankie Frisch, a grizzled veteran of the diamond wars, who came to the cards from the Giants as a second baseman in 1927 and who took over as manager in mid-season 1933, loved Dizzy like an errant kid brother.

As Frankie went through the travails of trying to lead his team to a pennant with Dean as the ace of his pitching staff, he experi-enced a variety of emotions—he suffered and sweated and wept and rejoiced—sometimes all on the same day. Frisch continuously tried to tell Diz how to pitch to enemy batters but without much success. Several times, for example, old "Fordham Flash" Frankie would walk toward the mound from his second base position to offer a pitching tip, but Dean would haughtily wave him away.

Matters came to a head on September 21, 1934 when Dizzy and Paul were slated to go up against the Brooklyn Dodgers in a late-season doubleheader. In the clubhouse before the start of the twin bill, Frisch went through the Brooklyn lineup, painstakingly trying to explain to Dizzy how to "feed 'em to the hitters." Diz came out with either a grunt of a wisecrack for each tip. He finally held up his hand and broke into this instructional session with these remarks.

"Now listen here, Frankie…. I've won twenty-six games so far this season and it don't look right for no infielder to be tellin' a star like me how to pitch a game o' ball."

Frisch blew his top and looked as if he were going to belt his ace pitcher, but Dean only grinned broadly.

"Aw, now, Frankie," he countered good-naturedly, "don't get so excited. I doubt if them Dodgers get a hit off'n me or Paul this afternoon."

Dizzy happened to be in top form that day and held Brooklyn hitless through the first seven innings. With two out in the eighth, the Dodgers got their first hit of the game and Dean had to settle for a three-hit shutout. Then Paul took over in the next game and, amazingly enough, threw a no-hitter!"

Dizzy, who was clearly upstaged by his brother, told reporters: "I wish I'd a known he was goin' to pitch a no-hitter today. I would of, too."

After this memorable day, Frankie Frisch rarely offered any pitching advice to either of the Deans.

The Dean brothers went on to become even bigger heroes in the '34 World Series against the Detroit Tigers. In that dramatic seven-game set St. Louis whipped the hard-hitting Tigers four games to three, with the Deans gaining credit for all the Cards victories: Dizzy finished with a Series record of 2-1 and a 1.73 ERA, and Daffy topped that with a 2-0 mark and a 1.00 ERA.

◆

FREAK INJURY

DIZZY AND DAFFY HAD a strong season again in 1935, winning twenty-eight and nineteen games, respectively, and though the Cardinals finished with an excellent 96-58 record, the Chicago Cubs edged them out for the pennant by a four-game margin. Paul's arm went bad after the '35 season. Then Dizzy's career took a sharp nosedive as the result of an injury in the 1937 All-Star Game.

Staged at Griffith Stadium, Washington, D.C., the All-Star was preceded by elaborate pre-game ceremonies which featured President Franklin D. Roosevelt being driven out onto the field in an open car. An array of Cabinet officers, members of Congress, foreign diplomats, and assorted dignitaries were also in the box seats. A large delegation of Boy Scouts, attending the first National Jamboree in Washington, assisted in the impressive flag-raising.

For the first two frames the game was ita pitchers' battle as Lefty Gomez (New York Yankees) and Dizzy Dean, making his second consecutive start for the N.L. (Diz was the winning pitcher in the '36 game), completed shutout innings.

Dean retired the first two batters in the third, but then Joe DiMaggio banged out his first All-Star hit, a line single. Lou Gehrig was the next batter up. Dean ran the count to 3-and-2 and then shook off a call by catcher Gabby Hartnett. Gehrig in 1937 was still at the peak of his brilliant career, and was no man to fool with. But the cocky Dean foolishly challenged him by throwing to his strength. Unloading a fastball instead of a sharp breaker, Dean watched Gehrig blast it way over the right-field fence, a wallop that measured some 450 feet.

Obviously miffed with himself, Dizzy next tried to fog one past

Earl Averill (Cleveland Indians). Averill, the "Rock of Snohomish," was expecting this fast one and rifled it back to the box. The ball struck Dean on the left foot and bounded away. Dean chased it down and nipped Averill at first on a close play, but when he reached the clubhouse he discovered his big toe was broken.

That play proved to be the turning point in Dean's career. He began pitching again long before the injury was healed completely. In doing so he was forced to change his motion and that placed an unnatural strain on his right arm and shoulder. Bursitis developed and he lost his great speed.

DIZZY WAS TRADED TO THE CUBS in 1938 and helped them win a pennant with a 7-1 record as a spot pitcher, but he had to depend on his new "dipsey doodle" pitch and sheer cunning. After that he hung on for a while, but by the time he was thirty his big league days were over—he was retired because of his lame arm. He struggled but he never came close to regaining the fastball which had terrified batters.

Jim "Doc" Ewell, who had spent more than thirty-five years as a big league trainer before retiring in 1979, talked about the strange case of Dizzy Dean in depth:

"Dean, unfortunately, took the old hard-nosed attitude and made the cardinal error of getting back into action long before he was physically ready. We really can't blame Dizzy for that catastrophic mistake. It just wasn't the fashion in those day to sit out too many games with an injury. . . .the idea was to grab a bat or a glove and run out onto the field, no matter what.

"Don't forget that Dean was only twenty-six at the time of that freak accident, and you'd assume that the club management also had a responsibility to keep a close eye on his during the recovery process. However, I doubt we'll see Dizzy Dean-type cases today because we've added a lot of sophistication to our training techniques.

"Nowadays if a star pitcher like Roger Clemens comes up with the slightest twinge in his arm or shoulder, trainers rush over to him like a rescue squad, and the managers and coaches won't let him pitch until he's 100 percent right. Pitchers in convalescence today can't even pick up a ball without getting permission. They always have a coach tailing them. If a pitching coach had really looked closely at Dean trying to throw after that All-Star Game, he would have known something was radically wrong.

"WHEN I WAS THE CHIEF TRAINER with the Houston Astros, we never let a superstar like Cesar Cedeno, or any other player, get into a game unless he was physically right. Why should a ballclub take needless chances with multimillion-dollar ballplayers? It's crazy to play hurt and ruin a career.

"Sure, Dizzy Dean won 150 games in the majors, but if he had been made to wait a whole lot longer after getting hit by the batted ball, maybe he could have won three-hundred. To be brutally frank, big league baseball fifty years ago was in many ways run in a primitive style as compared with modern standards."

Dean's final big league stats came to 150 wins, 83 losses for a winning percentage of .644 and an ERA of 3.03, good enough to gain him Hall of Fame election in 1953. Interestingly, Paul won fifty games in his career (to go with thirty-four losses), so the two brothers managed to win exactly two-hundred games between them, though they were cut down by those terrible arm problems when they were still flowering as super-pitchers. Dizzy's total of 150 victories is the fewest of any Hall of Famer. Paul, like Dizzy, tried several comebacks and failed each time.

About the time that Dizzy Dean was being enshrined in the Hall of Fame, Hollywood tried to capture him on film in a movie titled *The Pride of St. Louis*, with actor Dan Dailey starring in the role as "Ol' Diz." Bosley Crowther wrote in his review in *The New York Times*

"The magnetic thing is the nature of a great, big lovable lug who plays baseball for a living and lives just to play—or talk—baseball. It is not Dizzy Dean the Cardinal pitcher, the powerhouse of the old Gashouse Gang, the man who won so many games in so many seasons, that is the hero of this film. It is Dizzy Dean the character, the whiz from the Ozark hills, the braggart, the woeful grammarian, the humble human being."

◆

LEFTY GROVE'S TEMPER

ROBERT MOSES ("LEFTY") GROVE was as well known for his hot temper as for his brilliant pitching in a major league career that spanned seventeen seasons (1925-41). Lefty won exactly three-hundred games and lost only 141, good for a lofty winning percentage of .680. Moreover, he fashioned a lifetime ERA of 3.06 in an era when hitters dominated the game. He led the American League for the lowest ERA in a record nine seasons.

Grove spent the first nine years of his big league career with the Philadelphia Athletics and the remaining eight with the Boston Red Sox.

Born in a small town in the Appalachian Mountain country of Western Maryland, Grove developed a suspicious nature and a mean disposition. While with the Athletics, he gave Connie Mack, one of the gentlest of all managers, the absolute fits.

Grove, as the ace of the Athletics pitching staff, felt privileged to be the only player on the team to call the venerable manager

"Connie." To everyone else on staff, it had to be "Mr. Mack."

When trying for his seventeenth consecutive victory in 1931, which would have been a new American League record, Grove lost the game by a 1-0 count to St. Louis when left-fielder Jim Moore misjudged a fly ball, allowing the lone run to score.

After the defeat, Grove charged into the clubhouse like a mad bull. He slammed doors, kicked the water pail, threw his spikes into the locker, and roared. When his catcher Mickey Cochrane said, "Hard luck, Lefty," he unleashed a torrent of profanity that sent Mickey retreating and mumbling to himself.

When Connie Mack entered the clubhouse, the manager employed some of the strongest language he ever used in trying to quiet down the volcanic Grove when he said, "Shut up, Robert."

When that had no effect, Mack took the problem in hand further. He tried to solve the situation, not by pitying Grove, but by praising Browns righthander Dick Coffman, who had allowed the A's only three hits. "Robert, didn't Coffman pitch a wonderful game today? We only got 3 singles and we wouldn't have scored a run if we had still been playing."

Grove, now struggling to control his anger, agreed at least that Coffman deserved to win. That calmed him down.

When Lefty Grove joined the Red Sox, he was approaching his mid-thirties, but his disposition was just as nasty as ever. He certainly wasn't mellowing with age. One time in a 1935 game at Detroit, shortstop-manager Joe Cronin tried to stop a hot smash off the bat of Hank Greenberg by getting down on one knee so that he could at least trap the ball. The ball struck Cronin on the knee cap and ricocheted off into left-center-field.

"Okay, Cronin, get up off your knees and field your position like a man!" he screamed from the pitcher's mound. Grove could have waited to get into the dugout or clubhouse to chastise

Cronin for the misplay which allowed two runs to score and cost Grove the game.

In Cronin's defense, it should be pointed out that the vogue in those days was for infielder to get down on one knee—or on both knees—to field sizzling ground balls. You won't see infielding of that type very often today.

◆

BALLSY ROOKIES

"WHO'S THE GUTSIEST PLAYER you've ever seen perform on a baseball diamond?" asked a grizzled scout during an informal discussion among veteran baseball men at Oakland's Alameda County Stadium before the start of the 1987 All-Star Game.

Another senior scout with decades of experience to his credit got up and answered without a second's hesitation, "That player, in my estimation, has got to be Eddie Mathews." He then went on to give specifics along these lines.

Mathews, a left-handed power-hitting third baseman came up to the Boston Braves as a twenty-year-old rookie in 1952, and National League pitchers went all out immediately to test his mettle. In one of his first big league games, Mathews faced big right-handed fastball hurler Herman Wehmeier of the Cincinnati Reds at Crosley Field. Wehmeier had a reputation for wildness, having already led the league in walks twice, and in '52 he was on his way to leading the circuit in that department again. He also had the reputation of being a "head-hunter."

Wehmeier's first pitch was a blazing high inside fastball that went straight at Mathews's head, but Eddie instinctively dropped to the ground in a heap to avoid being decapitated. He dusted himself off, and got right back into the batter's box. Wehmeier's second pitch speeded in at the same spot and again Mathews fell to the ground. After he dusted himself off, he clenched his teeth in fierce determination, dug himself a firm toehold at the plate, and waited for another delivery. This time the pitch came straight down the middle; Eddie caught hold of it squarely and whacked a vicious line drive that went far over the right-field wall for a homer—the first of his career.

From that moment on, National League moundsmen grew to respect Eddie Mathews. In all, Mathews slammed out 512 homers in his seventeen years in the majors, and one of the biggest had to be that shot off Herm Wehmeier at the very dawn of his career. It didn't surprise anyone that he was eventually elected to the Hall of Fame at Cooperstown.

◆

HUBBELL'S SCREWBALL

YOUNG CARL HUBBELL threw left-handed and batted right, pitched and played the outfield for the Meeker (Oklahoma) high school team when he wasn't busy with farm chores. It wasn't until he was all of twenty when he launched his pro career.

With Oklahoma City in 1925, Hubbell appeared in forty-five games, pitched 284 innings and finished at 17-13. The Detroit Tigers, thinking Hubbell showed some promise for all his frail appearance, bought his contract and invited him to spring training in 1926.

Ty Cobb, then managing Detroit, was not overly impressed with Carl's work, and had him shipped off to Toronto of the Class AA International League where he compiled a mediocre 7-7 record. Hubbell appeared at spring training with the Tigers again in 1927 and the new manager, George Moriarty, was impressed even less and sent Carl down to Decatur, Illinois, of the Class B Three-Eye League. At Decatur he fashioned an excellent 14-7 record with a very low 2.53 ERA.

It was along about here that Hubbell, now 24, realizing he was going nowhere, began tinkering with the screwball. John Drebinger, who covered Hubbell's entire career for *The New York Times*, said: "It intrigued Carl's studious nature to see batters become hopelessly confused by a pitch that curved one way when they expected it to go the other."

When Tiger manager Moriarty inspected Hub's screwball again in spring training 1928, he declared: "Young man, if you persist in throwing that pitch, your days in baseball are numbered. It is certain to ruin your arm."

And with that the Tigers sold Hubbell outright to Beaumont of the Texas League, without having used him in a single championship game in a Detroit uniform.

Relying on his newly refined screwball, Hubbell blossomed at Beaumont as he went 12-9 by mid-season with a 2.97 ERA. He managed to control his pet pitch almost perfectly as he walked only forty-five and struck out 116 in 185 innings of work.

THE NEW YORK GIANTS, desperately in need of pitching to stay in the National League pennant race, took note of these happenings, and bought Hubbell's contract from Beaumont in mid-July for $40,000, a big chunk of cash in those days. Under Giants manager John McGraw's direction, Hub finished the '28 season with a strong 10-6 (ERA 2.83) mark.

The Giants ultimately closed out the season in second place, just two games behind pennant-winning St. Louis, with Manager McGraw observing with regret: "If Carl Hubbell had started out the year with us, we would have finished first easily."

Curiously enough, George Moriarty's prediction that the screwball would ruin Hubbell's arm proved to be correct. Throwing a pitch like that places enormous stress on the arm, especially on and around the elbow region. When Hub retired after the 1943 season, his left arm was grotesquely bent out of shape; it looked like scythe hanging down from his side. "I would have liked to pitch a while longer, but it was tough throwing a ball with a crooked arm," he said later.

However, in those sixteen seasons with the Giants he had established himself as one of the greatest left-handers in baseball history. Hubbell won 253, lost 154 for a winning percentage of .622, and he fashioned a skinny 2.98 ERA in this heavy-hitting era. In three World Series (1933, 1936—37), "King Carl" went 4-2, compiling a 1.79 ERA in fifty innings of work.

He set a modern major league record when he won twenty-four straight gams: sixteen for the last half of the '36 season and eight more at the start of the '37 campaign. He won more than twenty games in five successive seasons (1933-37), reaching a high-water mark in 1936 with a glittering 26-6 posting.

Hubbell, known as "the Meal Ticket" because of his reliability, enjoyed his greatest moments of all, perhaps, in the 1934 All-Star Game at the Polo Grounds when he struck out five of the greatest sluggers in American League history in succession: Babe Ruth, Lou Gehrig, Jimmie Foxx, Al Simmons and Joe Cronin (all five are in baseball's Hall of Fame.)

VERNON "LEFTY" GOMEZ, another great southpaw, explained how Hubbell's screwball worked in these terms: "Carl was a pitcher's pitcher...we all admired him because he had absolute powers of concentration while working, and he had persevered for years to master pinpoint control.

"Hub's type of screwball is a pitch thrown with a reverse twist of the wrist which makes the ball break in a direction opposite to that of a normally thrown curveball. Since Carl was a southpaw, the pitch broke in toward a left-handed batter instead of away from him—then against a right-handed hitter, the ball broke away from him instead of in to him. Hubbell was especially tough against right-handed swingers who would normally expect to murder a southpaw curve baller.

"No one had thrown the so-called 'fadeaway' pitch, or 'reverse curve,' so effectively since Christy Mathewson and he was a right-hander.

"Carl ordinarily relied on his screwball in clutch situations only…if he threw it all the time, batters would have gotten used to it and belt the ball all over the lot." But the pitch was new to the American Leaguers in that 1934 All-Star Game, and old Hub got them all tied up in knots.

Lefty Gomez himself was quite a comic. His nemesis was the big Red Sox slugger Jimmie Foxx. Gomez said, "He has muscles in his hair." During one game with Bill Dickey catching, Gomez kept shaking off Dickey's signals. Finally, Bill ran out to the mound and said, "What do you want to throw?"

"I don't wanna throw nothin'," Gomez said. "Maybe he'll get tired of waiting and leave."

◆

HAPPY MOTHER'S DAY, MA!

IT WAS A WARM MOTHER'S DAY, May 14, 1939, almost cloudless throughout much of the Midwest, and an ideal day for baseball.

Bob Feller, the twenty-year-old fireballing phenom for the Cleveland Indians, was scheduled to face the Chicago White Sox at Comisky Park—and for the occasion Feller's family, including his father, mother, and eight-year-old sister, Marguerite, decided to drive from their homestead in Van Meter, Iowa, to Chicago, a distance of some 250 miles, to see the game.

The Fellers found themselves comfortably ensconced in grandstand seats between home and first base just before game time, and they watched as the Indians scored two runs in the first inning and four more in the third to take a 6-0 lead. Rapid Robert Feller was in rare form as he blanked the White Sox for the first two innings, not allowing a hit.

In the bottom of the third, Chicago third baseman Marvin Owen, a pinch hitter, had trouble getting around on Feller's ninety-nine-mile-an-hour fastball as he sent three straight soft fouls into the stands between first and home. On the next pitch, Owen swung late again, but this time he got the barrel of the bat on the ball and sent a vicious foul liner to the first base stands again—and to the exact spot where the Feller party was seated. There was no time to duck, and, tragically, the ball struck Mrs. Feller in the face.

As Feller followed through with his pitching motion, he could see clearly that his mother was struck by the ball. In recalling the incident years later, Feller said, "I felt sick, but I saw that Mother was conscious...I saw the police and ushers leading her out and I had to put down the impulse to run to the stands. Instead, I kept on pitching. I felt giddy and I became wild and couldn't seem to find the plate. I know the Sox scored three runs, but I'm not sure how.

"They immediately told me the injury was painful but not serious. There wasn't anything I could do, so I went on and finished the game and won. Then I hurried to the hospital.

"Mother looked up from the hospital bed, her face bruised and both eyes blacked, and she was still able to smile reassuringly.

"My head aches, Robert,' she said, 'but I'm all right. Now don't go blaming yourself…it wasn't your fault.'"

Mrs. Feller spent a couple of days in the hospital and was released feeling no ill effects.

The Indians won that Mother's Day game 9-4 as Feller ran his record to 6-1. For the entire season he went 24-9 and struck out a major league-leading 246 batters.

In his autobiography *Strikeout Story*, Feller emphasized that his mother was always a good soldier who helped to advance his baseball career in a thousand different ways.

Feller also said later: "It was a one-in-a-million shot that my own mother while sitting within a crowd of people at a ballpark would be struck by a foul ball resulting from a pitch I made." And on Mother's Day.

◆

COBB AND SISLER

ON OCTOBER 4, 1925, fans saw the unusual spectacle of two managers, both renowned hitters, PITCH against each other in the season's finale. Right-hander Ty Cobb of the Detroit Tigers hurled one perfect inning and left-hander George Sisler of the St. Louis Browns worked two scoreless innings in an 11-6 Tiger victory. Neither Cobb nor Sisler figured in the decision.

Cobb, who occasionally threw batting practice, had pitched 4 innings in a couple of games for the Tigers back in 1918—and that was the extent of his mound experience.

"GOOFY" GOMEZ

VERNON "LEFTY" GOMEZ, one of the most colorful players in big league history, anchored the New York Yankees pitching staff during the 1930s as he became a twenty-game winner four times and wound up with an imposing 189-102 career record. Moreover, he won six World Series games without a loss (a record) and went 3-1 in 1930s All-Star competition. He was elected to the Hall of Fame in 1972.

No matter how critical the situation became on the baseball field, Lefty never lost his sharp sense of humor, and because of his constant practical joking he became known as "El Goofo" or just plain "Goofy" Gomez.

GOMEZ'S MOST MEMORABLE GOOF occurred during the second game of the 1936 World Series against the hard-hitting New York Giants at the Polo Grounds.

More than fifty years after this episode Gomez remembered it well as he related:

"It was early in the game, I was a little wild, and before I knew it there were two runners on base. Suddenly I heard a plane flying over the ball park—it was a big airliner—and I just stepped off the mound, forgot about the runners, the batter, the game and everything else. I stood there watching calmly until the plane completely disappeared from sight.

"Sure, I kept 45,000 fans (as well as the players) waiting and everyone wondered why I stopped the game this way...some people thought I was just plain crazy. Well, I was a little tense and I wanted to ease the tension a bit. As I recall, I came out of that inning pretty well unscathed."

The Yankees went on to whip the Giants by a whopping 18 to 4 as Gomez went the distance, walking seven and striking out eight.

The mists of antiquity may have settled a bit on the details of that game, but Lefty Gomez will always be remembered as the player who stopped the World Series dead in its tracks to watch an airplane in flight.

After Lefty Gomez finished recalling the 1936 World Series he went on to reminisce:

"Certainly one of my greatest moments in baseball came in the spring of 1930 when I first got into the big leagues with the New York Yankees and became a teammate of Babe Ruth. Ruth was the greatest single character I ever came in contact with. On the ball field he was a genius…there wasn't anything he couldn't do.

"One time, in about the summer of 1932, he was out at an all-night formal party and came into the Yankees clubhouse in his tuxedo, without having so much as a wink of sleep. As soon as he began putting on his uniform his eyes began to clear up, and that afternoon he led the Yankees to a victory over the White Sox by smashing a couple of homers."

◆

THE KING OF ZING

NOLAN RYAN IN 1987, at the age of forty and in his twentieth year in the major leagues, enjoyed one of his finest seasons on the mound despite the fact that he went 8-16 for the Houston Astros. Regardless of that losing record, the right-handed fireballer led the National League in strikeouts with 270 and in ERA with a very low 2.7. Since Ryan pitched only 212 innings, he averaged more than eleven strikeouts per game.

Up to this point, any pitcher who has led the National League in both strikeouts and ERA has taken the Cy Young award. Ryan didn't win the 1987 Cy Young award because of the 8-16 posting, but many baseball observers strongly felt he should have received it despite the .333 won-lost percentage. In those sixteen losses, the weak-hitting Astros scored exactly twelve runs while Ryan was on the mound. Nolan should have "sued' his teammates for nonsupport.

Though Nolan Ryan has reached an age when most other pitchers survive by resorting to knuckleballs, spitballs, sandpaper, or prayer, he seems to have lost little or nothing on his fastball as he consistently throws in the high 90s. He remains the king of zing. His changeup, according to Los Angeles Dodgers speed-gun operator Mike Brito, clocks in at eighty-seven or eighty-eight miles per hour, a bit faster than Fernando Valenzuela's fastball.

"No one throws as fast as Ryan," said Dodgers infielder Phil Garner. "Dwight Gooden of the Mets throws the ball real good, but it doesn't explode on you like Nolan's. His looks like it picks up speed as it comes to the plate."

Ryan's 4,547 lifetime strikeouts through 1987 are far and away a major league record and he looks forward to pitching at least several more years in the majors—and run his K total up to five-thousand, an astounding number.

"Certainly 1987 was an unusual year for me since I won only eight games despite all those strikeouts and a low ERA, but there are some things in baseball you just can't explain," Ryan told reporters at season's end.

This writer interviewed Nolan Ryan in March, 1985, in Florida before a spring-training game and asked: "How is it that you've been able to maintain your great speed in your late thirties while most power pitchers lose their velocity fairly early in their careers?"

Ryan answered without batting an eye: "I guess it must be because I'm from Texas." Ryan, a native of Refugio, Texas, makes his home in Alvin, a few miles south of Houston, where he engages in cattle breeding and in banking.

◆

THE FASTEST PITCHER?

ACCORDING TO THE *Guinness Book of World Records*, at one time the fastest recorded major league pitcher was Nolan Ryan, who, on August 20, 1974, while with the California Angels, threw a pitch at Anaheim Stadium, California, measured at 100.9 miles per hour.

Steve Dalkowski, little-known lefthander (born June 3, 1939), though not generally regarded as the fastest pitcher in baseball history, threw a pitch measured at 108 miles per hour while with Elmira in the Class A Eastern League in 1962.

Dalkowski spent nine years in the minor leagues (1957-65), mostly as a Baltimore Orioles farmhand, reaching as high as Rochester and Columbus of the International League, but his wildness prevented his promotion to the majors. He was invited to spring training several times by the Orioles, but never reached his true potential though he possessed an enormous amount of raw talent.

In those nine years in the minors, Dalkowski put together one of the strangest pitching records in professional baseball history. Over the course of 236 games, he posted a 46-80 won-lost record (.366 percentage) and pitched 995 innings, allowing only 682 base hits. He walked the Gargantuan total of 1,354 batters and struck out an equally Gargantuan 1,396. His ERA was a rather bloated 5.59.

Thus, in a typical game Dalkowski gave up six hits, walked

twelve and struck out twelve to thirteen. If he went the distance, his game almost always took more than three hours to complete, and no one who ever paid his way into a game pitched by Steve Dalkowski ever complained about not getting his money's worth. Every game he pitched as a dramatic event.

While with Stockton of the Class A California League in 1960, he pitched 170 innings in thirty-two games, won seven games, lost fifteen, allowed only 105 hits, walked 262, and struck out 262! Obviously he was very hard to hit.

Dalkowski's great left arm began giving out before he was twenty-seven, and from that point on, his journey through life was not altogether happy. He worked for a time as a migratory laborer in California's vineyards and had long bouts with John Barleycorn.

In 1978, the Society for American Baseball Research (then based in Cooperstown, New York) honored Dalkowski by including him in a newly published biographical and statistical volume entitled *All-Time Minor League Baseball Stars*.

◆

SPITBALL PITCHER

AFTER BURLEIGH GRIMES ENDED his active career in the majors, he became player-manager for Bloomington in the Three-I League in 1935. Burleigh was barely at the midpoint of his professional baseball career at this juncture. He managed Louisville in the American Association in 1936 and then he led the Brooklyn Dodgers in 1937-38. Grimes held the reins at Brooklyn between the manager tenures of Casey Stengel and Leo Durocher.

After directing Montreal in the International League in 1939,

Grimes somehow went down a couple of steps on the managerial ladder in 1940 when he was named pilot of Grand Rapids in the Class C Michigan State League. And it was in his Grand Rapids tenure that he endured the worst experience in his professional baseball career spanning nearly three-score years.

In early July, Grimes took his Grand Rapids Colts down to Flint for a crucial game in the Michigan State League pennant race, but from the very start Burleigh became dissatisfied with the calls of home plate umpire Bob Williams. Toward the late innings, Grimes could take it no more and embroiled himself in a violent argument with Williams. In fact, the old spitballer became so exasperated that he ran out of words and vented his anger and spat out his entire chaw of tobacco smack into Williams's face.

Williams, naturally enough, promptly ejected Grimes from the game, and a few days later, on July 7, Judge William G. Bramham, president of the National Association of Professional Baseball Leagues (the governing body of minor league baseball) did Williams one better by suspending Grimes for an entire year.

The suspension took effect from the date of the offense and thus any plans Grimes had for managing in 1941 had to be scrapped. In being banished from organized baseball for a full year, Grimes took the stiffest punishment a manager had ever received up to that point. (In September 1942, Judge Bramham suspended manager Ben Chapman of Richmond in the Piedmont League for a full year for slugging an umpire.)

Grimes, who fought the suspension, had plenty of support from his many friends in baseball, and during the lengthy hearings on the case, umpire Bob Williams was suspended for "inefficiency" and "for the good of the league," but he was later reinstated in good standing.

In recalling the incident more than forty years later, Grimes, as he sat in a comfortable easy chair in the Otesaga lobby, said softly: "It was a hot day, the game was going badly, the umpire, in my estimation, was making a lot of bad calls, and I just lost my head momentarily. I shouldn't have done it…and it really cost me."

Grimes, professional all the way, got back into the game in 1942 as manager of Toronto in the International League for the first of his three tours of duty there: 1942-44, 1947 and 1952-53. He managed Rochester, also in the I.L., in 1945-46, with his final assignment in uniform coming in 1955 when he coached the Kansas City Athletics.

Then he served several long stints as a scout for a number of teams, including the New York Yankees, Kansas City A's, and the Baltimore Orioles. The latter assignment stretched from 1960 to 1971, Burleigh's last full-time job in baseball. He had made the rounds.

During the last dozen or so years of his long life, Burleigh Grimes worked actively on the Hall of Fame's Committee on Baseball Veterans, and enjoyed some of his best days holding court at the Otesaga lobby during Hall of Fame Induction Ceremony time. Reporters came flocking to him with pads, pencils, and tape recorders to seek his views on everything from the art of throwing the spitball to historic games he was involved in generations ago.

Hall of Famer Burleigh Grimes, ordinarily a good-hitting pitcher, once made eight outs in a single game on only four at-bats—he hit into a triple play, two double plays, and struck out!

◆

THE FATHER OF THE SLIDER

GEORGE BLAEHOLDER RAN UP a mediocre 104-125 record as a

right-handed pitcher in the American League from 1925 to 1936, but he is credited with having been the first pitcher to throw the slider, one of the most difficult of all pitches to hit. He threw his first slider with the St. Louis Browns in 1928, and generously passed on his technique to other pitchers.

The slider takes off like a fastball, but then curves sharply just before it reaches the batter. Batters have scornfully referred to the slider as a "nickel curve." The pitch really didn't have a major impact upon baseball until the 1950s and 1960s.

Stan Musial, one of the greatest batters of all time (he banged out 3,630 base hits and averaged .331 in a twenty-three-year career, 1941-63), once said: "I could have hit better in the latter years of my career and stayed around a while longer if it hadn't been for the slider."

◆

"BOOM-BOOM"

IN AN ACTIVE BASEBALL CAREER that spanned twenty-seven years (1924-50), Walter "Boom-Boom" Beck, a native of Decatur, Illinois, spent a good deal of his time traveling as he pitched for a total of twenty-three teams in thirteen different leagues, including both major leagues. In addition to his American and National League experience, Beck toiled in the following circuits that are obscure to many fans: Three-I League, Texas Association, Western League, American Association, International League, Southern Association, Pacific Coast League, Inter-State League, Southeast League, Central League, and Middle Atlantic League. In the latter three leagues he was a player-manager.

As a major leaguer the right-handed-throwing Beck saw action with the St. Louis Browns, Brooklyn Dodgers, Philadelphia Phillies, Detroit Tigers, Cincinnati Reds, and Pittsburgh Pirates, and posted a 38-69 record in 265 games. In the minors, he went 199-167, making his total pro regular season record come to just one victory over .500, or 237-236.

Beck enjoyed his finest season in the minors with the Memphis Chicks in 1932 when he rolled up an impressive 27-6 mark to rank as the leading pitcher in the Southern Association. This earned him a return trip to the big leagues in 1933, this time with Brooklyn, and it was in Flatbush that Beck earned his unusual nickname.

While pitching against the Phillis on a sweltering 1934 afternoon in Philadelphia's Baker Bowl, Beck was removed from the game by manager Casey Stengel while still holding a slim lead. Losing his cool, Beck wound up and threw the ball with all his strength toward right-field where it made a resounding "boom" as it struck the tin fence. Outfielder Hack Wilson, who had not been paying attention during the pitching change, heard the "boom" and, thinking the ball was in play, fielded it and made a perfect line throw to second base. This unusual episode caused all the fans and players, except for Beck, to laugh heartily. From that time on Walter Beck was known as "Boom-Boom." Hack Wilson, a Hall of Famer who had his best season in the majors with the Chicago Cubs when he hit fifty-six homers and knocked in 190 runs (the all-time major league record), was then in the twilight of his career and found himself released by the Dodgers to the Phillies later in the 1934 season.

After his playing days were over, "Boom-Boom" Beck remained in baseball for another two decades as a coach and scout at both the major and minor league levels. He died at Champaign, Illinois, on May 7, 1987, at the age of eighty-two.

DON'T MESS WITH EARLY

EARLY WYNN, THE HALL OF FAME right-hander who piled up a 300-244 won-lost record over twenty-three big league seasons (1939-63, with time out for World War II service), looked as mean as a junkyard dog when he took the mound. Most batters were afraid to dig in on "Burley Early" because they never knew when his brushback pitch was coming.

One reporter commented that Early would knock down his own grandmother if she ever crowded the plate—fortunately, she never had the opportunity of batting against her grandson. However, when Early was nearing the end of the trail with the Chicago White Sox in the early 1960s, he pitched against his seventeen-year-old son Early, Jr., in batting practice. Well, Early, Jr., socked one of his dad's best pitches up against the bleacher wall. What do you suppose happened when the boy dug in for his father's next delivery? He was sent flying on his derriere, of course, in order to avoid the high hard one.

ALEXANDER THE GREAT

EARLY IN THE 1996 SEASON, the Texas Rangers crushed the Baltimore Orioles by a score of 26-7, with all of the twenty-six runs being earned. In the eighth inning alone, the Rangers scored sixteen times as Oriole pitching dished up ninety-nine juicy pitches to the salivating sluggers during the seemingly endless frame.

Desperate for another pitcher, Baltimore took utility infielder Manny Alexander off the bench put him out on the mound. He gave up four walks and a grand slam while toiling just two-thirds of an inning.

That prompted Orioles announcing and ex-pitcher Mike Flanagan to deadpan, "There are some great pitching Alexanders in baseball history: Grover Cleveland Alexander, Doyle Alexander, and now, Manny Alexander."

◆

PITCHER TURNED SLUGGER

WHEN THE 1997 SEASON opened, Chicago Cubs center fielder Brian McRae felt safe concerning a promise he had made three years earlier. He had told teammate Frank Castillo he would buy him a Mercedes Benz if Castillo, a pitcher and notoriously poor hitter, could ever swat a home run (even during batting practice).

Well, on May 30 Castillo, a 1.08 hitter, went deep twice during his round in the batting cage prior to a game. This hitting display pleased the man who normally couldn't hit a lick, but brought dismay and utter disbelief to McRae. When asked what he made of the whole situation, McRae simply stated, "He's still the worst hitting pitcher I've ever seen!"

◆

MULLHOLLAND'S MITT MAGIC

AFTER WATCHING BASEBALL for decades, many fans come to believe that they've seen it all. In reality, the nature of baseball is such that about the time you become blasé, something odd will come along to make you shout, "Wow!"

One such play occurred on September 3, 1986, when a San Francisco Giants rookie pitcher named Terry Mulholland made an amazing fielding play. He was facing the New York Mets in the third inning when he stabbed a hard grounder off the bat of Keith Hernandez.

It turned out the Mets All-Star had drilled the ball so hard, it became lodged in Mulholland's glove. The southpaw hurler tried to pull the ball loose, but he also realized time was running out, and Hernandez would soon reach base safety. So, he trotted a few strides toward first base, gave up on freeing the ball, removed his glove (the ball still nestled inside), and tossed the glove to the first baseman, Bob Brenly. The umpire didn't miss a beat as he correctly ruled that Hernandez was out in a truly bizarre play.

◆

PITCHERS' HUMOR

ANOTHER HALL OF FAMER, fireballing "Bullet" Bob Gibson of the St. Louis Cardinals, was also highly intense. At one time, only Walter Johnson had fanned more batters than Gibson. In 1968, Gibson stunned the baseball world with his microscopic ERA of 1.12, helped greatly by an incredible thirteen shutouts. As a student of the game, he once observed, "A great catch is like watching girls go by. The last one you see is always the prettiest."

When Mike Scott and Nolan Ryan were both with the Houston Astros, Scott liked to get an occasional dig in on the aging veteran nicknamed the Ryan Express. One day after a game in which the Astros drew a meager crowd, Scott waited for the reporters to circle him near his locker. Then he unloaded with, "When I saw 1,938 (the number of people in attendance that was flashed on the scoreboard), I didn't know if it was the attendance or the year Ryan was born."

◆

AWARD-WINNING PERFORMANCE

IN A SPRING TRAINING GAME in the 1980s, the San Francisco Giants had Mike Krukow pitching. Suddenly after making a pitch, he howled in pain. The umpire, concerned for Krukow, allowed him to make a few practice tosses. After making the lobs, the pitcher said he felt he could stay in the game.

Krukow's very first pitch sailed wild, hitting the screen behind home plate. The next pitch didn't even come close to reaching the catcher.

Despite his apparent wildness, Krukow insisted he should face the next batter. He did and quickly retired the hitter by using duplicity. That is to say, Krukow wasn't in pain at all. Furthermore, due to the pitcher's theatrics, the batter wasn't ready to hit; he had been duped. Therefore, it wasn't surprising when Krukow's first offering was popped harmlessly to the infield, and the pitcher's fake grimace melted into a Cheshirelike grin.

◆

WHAT ARE THE ODDS?

JOE NIEKRO WAS A PITCHER for twenty-two seasons in the major leagues. While he did possess a splendid knuckleball, allowing him to chalk up 221 victories, he was certainly not much of a hitter. Throughout his career, he could muster just one home run (on May 29, 1976). What's so odd here is his only shot came against a fellow knuckleball artist who would wind up winning 318 games and who just happened to be Joe's brother, Phil.

◆

GO FIGURE

COUNTING PITCHERS who performed in the 1800s, there have been twenty men who have won three-hundred games or more. Exactly half of them never were able to hurl a no-hitter.

Huge stars such as Steve Carlton, Grover Alexander, Lefty Grove, and Early Wynn just could not come up with a "no-no." The combined win total of the ten greats who failed to throw a no-hitter is a staggering 3,268.

Yet, ironically, some little-known pitchers with very little talent somehow managed to achieve this. The most glaring example may well be that of Alva "Bobo" Holloman who threw a no-hitter in his first big league start for Bill Veeck's Browns in 1953. Just a short time later Holloman was gone from the big leagues forever. He wound up with a career mark of 3-7 and an inflated 5.23 ERA.

A Cincinnati pitcher by the name of Charles "Bumpus" Jones actually won less than Holloman (with a 2-4 record) yet also threw a no-hitter. It was his only victory that year and his only appearance. The following season he went 1-4 with an astronomical ERA or 10.19, marking his baseball demise.

Certainly, George Davis belongs on this list. He had a 1914 no-hitter for the Boston Braves and just six more wins over a mediocre 7-10 career.

Then there was Wilson Alvarez, who was the antithesis of Warren Spahn. Spahn had to wait until his sixteenth season when he was thirty-nine years old before he managed to put together a no-hitter. Alvarez, on the other hand, came up with his gem versus the Baltimore Orioles on August 11, 1991, as a twenty-one-year old member of the Chicago White Sox.

In fact, a few days before his gem, Alvarez was in the minor leagues at the Double-A level pitching for Birmingham. Then, in his Sox debut, and in just his second major-league start, he threw the no-hitter.

He was on fire that day, fanning the first three batters he faced to open the game, and the final hitter to wrap it up in style. The Venezuelan left-hander became the youngest no-hit artist since Vida Blue (eighty-six days younger) had thrown one in 1970.

◆

A BRAND-NEW PITCH

OATES WASN'T THE ONLY man to come up with a clever one-liner. During a Chicago-Cincinnati contest, Cubs relief pitcher Bob Patterson faced the always-tough Barry Larkin. The Cincinnati shortstop took Patterson deep for a tenth-inning, game-winning home run.

Later, when asked what pitch he had thrown, Patterson retorted, "It was a cross between a changeup and a screwball. It was a screwup."

FEARED FASTBALL ARTIST

WHEN SEATTLE'S RANDY JOHNSON threw his first big-league pitch back in 1988 as a member of the Montreal Expos, he automatically set a record. At six feet ten inches, he was the tallest pitcher in the history of the game. Before long, batters realized another fact about the southpaw: He threw about as hard as any man to ever toe the rubber.

One day in the Mariners clubhouse, the topic of firearms somehow came up. Johnson said he didn't own any, but felt that in a way he was armed and highly dangerous. He explained, "I keep a bag of baseballs near the bed. If someone breaks in, they better be wearing a batting helmet, because I'm going to throw at their heads."

◆

FIELDING

3

THE SPARROW

CHARLES DILLON "CASEY" STENGEL early in his career became renowned as one of baseball's true funny men—and one never knew when or where Stengel's ribald and irreverent sense of humor was going to break through.

After three years playing in the minors, Casey broke into the majors with the Brooklyn Dodgers at the tail end of the 1912 season. In his first game with the Dodgers, on September 17 against the Pittsburgh Pirates, Stengel enjoyed a banner day as he collected four singles and walked in five trips to the plate.

From that point on, Stengel became a Dodgers regular and in 1916 he played a key role in helping Brooklyn capture a pennant. Along the way he solidified his reputation as a prankster. Stengel became the bane of umpires and managers alike, with one of his favorite targets being Wilbert Robinson, the roly-poly pilot of the Dodgers.

One of Casey's pranks occurred at Daytona Beach, Florida, during spring training in 1915. On that occasion, Stengel was inspired by the recent feat of Washington catcher Gabby Street, who had caught a baseball dropped more than five-hundred feet from the top of the Washington Monument. The question now became: "Could a man catch a baseball dropped from an airplane?"

The airplane was supplied by Ruth Law, a noted pioneer woman flier, and the baseball was supplied by C.C. Stengel, except that it curiously became a grapefruit by the time it was dropped.

Stengel recalled: "Uncle Robbie was warming up this pitcher on the sidelines—we didn't have six coaches in those days. And this aviatrix—I believe it was the first one ever—flew over the dropped it. And Uncle Robbie saw it coming and waved everybody away like an outfielder and hollered, 'I've got it! I've got it!'

"Robbie got under this grapefruit, thinking it was a baseball, which hit him right on the pitcher's glove he put on, and the insides of it flew all over, seeds on his face and uniform, and flipped him right over on his back. Everybody came running up and commenced laughing, all except Robbie."

Before the beginning of the 1918 season, Stengel was traded to Pittsburgh and when Casey returned to Ebbets Field for the first time in an enemy uniform he was greeted by a rousing round of catcalls from the fans—and this inspired Casey to pull off one of his most fabled escapades.

When he was scheduled to bat for the first time, he marched up to home plate, bowed with exaggerated courtliness to the grandstand, doffed his cap—and out flew a sparrow. Casey had given them the bird!

On another occasion, as legend has it, he went out to right-field at Ebbets Field, spotted a drainage hole, and suddenly disappeared from sight. A few moments later he rose majestically, a manhole cover under his arm, just in time to catch a fly ball!

Later, when he became a hard-boiled manager, Stengel looked back on his wayward years as a rambunctious player and said:

"Now that I am a manager, I see the error of my youthful ways. If any player pulled that stuff on me now, I would probably fine his ears off."

Casey often spoke in a nonstop style that came to be known as "Stengelese"—a kind of convoluted double-talk laced with ambiguous antecedents, a lack of proper names (he generally referred to a player as "that guy"), and a liberal use of adjectives like "amazing" and "terrific."

He drew on baseball lore dating back to pre-World War I days, and would clinch points in rhetoric by declaring with finality: "You could look it up." And when a listener's attention waned, he would immediately recapture it by exclaiming, "Now, let me ask you," and would be off and running again.

Warren Spahn, who pitched for Casey Stengel at the beginning and end of his illustrious career (with the Boston Braves in 1942 and with the New York Mets in 1965) told this writer recently:

"Casey Stengel may have been a funny man in the eyes of the fans and sportswriters, but when you played for him you saw the real Casey. He was a tough and demanding manager. When he lectured us in the clubhouse or on the field there was nothing funny about him…he was all business. That's why he was a great manager. He had an amazingly deep knowledge of the game and his humor off the field was a kind of self-effacing cover."

◆

KILLER THROWS

SHERRY ROBERTSON, Washington Senators infielder during the 1940s, was noted for his strong but erratic throwing. One time, early in his career, during infield practice he uncorked a mighty throw from shortstop. The ball went way over the first baseman's head and struck and killed a fan seated in the first-base boxes. The incident was not ruled an error, but an accident.

◆

A CLASSIC COLLISION IN THE OUTFIELD

WHEN THIS WRITER was still in the primary grades, he saw one of his first big league games ever at Cleveland's Municipal Stadium on Sunday, June 23, 1940, as the Indians faced the Boston Red Sox.

In the eighth inning, Cleveland second baseman Ray Mack lined a drive deep into the left center-field gap, with center-fielder Doc Cramer and left-fielder Ted Williams converging on the ball. In their mad dash they didn't see each other, collided head-on, and were both knocked unconscious as the ball rolled to the gate at the 463-foot sign. Mack got an easy inside-the-park homer.

Cramer was the first to get up and after getting a whiff of smelling salts from the trainer he was able to continue on in the game, but poor Ted Williams was carried off the field on a stretcher and taken to a local hospital to have his fractured jaw repaired. "Ted the Kid" remained hospitalized for a couple of days and missed more than a week's worth of action.

IT WAS ALWAYS MY IMPRESSION that the collision was Cramer's fault because he was a twelve-year big league veteran and should have directed the play on Mack's drive, while Williams was only a twenty-two-year-old sophomore in the league at the time.

We finally got our chance to question Williams about the play forty-seven years after it happened, at the 1987 Hall of Fame Induction Ceremonies at Cooperstown. Williams said:

"Hell no, don't blame that collision on Cramer, it was my fault. I took off like crazy after Mack's liner and ran into Doc…if I left him alone, he would have had a good chance to flag it down. From that day on, I tried to look where I was going in the outfield."

◆

THE ONE-ARMED OUTFIELDER

GOOD BALLPLAYERS WERE extremely scarce during World War II, and the public, as well as the government, wanted baseball to carry on. The result was that many of the big leaguers of the 1942-45 period were those who were too young for the draft, or were classified 4-G (not physically fit for military duty).

The most famous 4-G of them all was one-armed outfielder Pete Gray, who had batted a solid .333 and had stolen sixty-eight bases for the Memphis Chicks in 1944, achievements that won him election as the Southern Association's Most Valuable Player. Gray became the talk of the big league world because his play in the S.A. was so impressive. The lowliest team, the St. Louis Browns, eagerly signed him for the 1945 campaign.

Gray had lost his right arm at the biceps in a boyhood accident, but he developed his left arm to such a degree and compensated for his handicap with such quickness that he became a really solid ballplayer. Gray had started out as a sandlot player in the Nanticoke, Pennsylvania, area as a teenager, and landed his first professional contract with Three Rivers, Ontario, of the Canadian-American League in 1942 at the age of twenty-five. From that point he moved up the minor league ladder rapidly.

This writer saw Gray in action several times with the Browns in 1945 and recalls vividly his performance against the Indians at Cleveland's Municipal Stadium in one particular four-game series in early June. Gray cracked out seven hits, including a triple and a double—both hard-hit line drives to deep left-center—in seventeen at-bats. Moreover, he fielded his left-field post flawlessly. After catching a fly ball, he would flip his glove under the stump of his right arm in a rapid-fire motion so that he could throw the ball with his bare left hand.

Gray batted only .218 in the tough American League competition. Amazingly enough, however, he struck out only eleven times in 234 official at-bats. When Gray took the field either in a minor or a major league park, no one ever did him any favors—he got along on his own grit. As a result, he became an inspiration during and after the war to the multitude of disabled U.S. war veterans.

Gray unfortunately found himself back in the minors once the war was over. He retired from active play after a season with Dallas of the Texas League in 1949.

◆

THE DISAPPEARING BASEBALL

IN 1958, LEON WAGNER was a raw rookie for the San Francisco Giants. During a July 1 contest, the opposing Chicago Cubs took advantage of his inexperience. Cubs batter Tony Taylor hit a shot to left field, where Wagner was stationed.

The ball bounded into the Cubs' bullpen before Wagner could track it down. He did notice, though, that the relief pitchers, who were viewing the game from that location, scattered. When those relievers stared under their bench, Wagner knew the ball had come to rest there.

He was wrong. He had been fooled by the enemy, who realized the ball had actually gone beyond the bullpen. In truth, the ball had come to a stop about forty-five feet further down the foul line. It was nestled in a rain gutter. By the time Wagner understood he had been faked out, Taylor had breezed around the bases for one of the oddest inside-the-park homers ever.

◆

POP-FLY BLOOPER

ARVEL ODELL "SAMMY" HALE, a hard-hitting infielder for the Cleveland Indians in the 1930s, had an affinity for a well-worn comfortable fielders' glove.

During a July 1939 game against the St. Louis Browns at Cleveland's League Park, Hale, playing second base, settled under an easy high pop fly. There were two men on and two out and the inning should have ended—if Sammy had made the catch.

Strangely enough, however, the ball dropped through Sammy's glove and two runs scored as a result of the error. Those two runs turned out to be the margin of victory for the Brownies.

It seems the ball dropped right through the webbing of Hale's battered old glove. The webbing was so worn out that it simply fell apart under the impact of the ball.

After the muff, Oscar Vitt, the Indians' manager, remarked in exasperation, "'Bout time to get a new glove, Sammy!"

Baseball players a generation or two ago usually hung on to their fielders' gloves for as long as possible. For one thing, they liked the feel of a well-worn glove, believing they could catch balls more easily with them. Then, the glove was the only piece of equipment that players had to buy for themselves, and they wouldn't spend money for a new one until it was absolutely necessary.

Lou Boudreau, Cleveland Indians shortstop, for example, used the same glove into the early 1940s that he had used when playing college ball for the University of Illinois in 1936-37. After relying on that one glove for seven or eight years, Boudreau broke down and bought another.

"That old fielder's mitt was like a part of the family, but I couldn't repair it anymore and it was falling apart on me," said Boudreau.

BREAKING BONES

THE 1950 ALL-STAR GAME, played on July 11, returned to Chicago's Comisky park where the interleague series had begun back in 1933.

In the first inning, Ralph Kinder (Pittsburgh Pirates) caught hold of a Vic Rasche (Yankees) fastball and lined a drive to deep left-center-field. Ted Williams (Boston Red Sox) raced back and made a spectacular one-handed catch, but in doing so he banged hard into the wall. Despite considerable pain in his left elbow, he remained in the game until the ninth inning.

Ted, of course, didn't realize it at the time but X-rays taken the next day showed a fracture; an operation was necessary, and Ted was sidelined until early September. However, in the All-Star Game, Ted continued to roam the outfield and swing away at the plate. In the bottom of the fifth inning, Williams, broken elbow and all, smacked a sharp single to right scoring Larry Doby (Cleveland Indians) to give the A.L. a 3-2 lead. By the ninth, however, the pain became so intense that Williams asked manager Casey Stengel to remove him from the game. The National League won the game in the 14th inning when Red Schoendienst's (St. Louis Cardinals) homer made the final score 4-3.

Ralph Kiner, now a television broadcaster for the New York Mets, commented recently on Williams's performance in the 1950 All-Star Game: "Ted robbed me of a sure extra base hit that day in Comiskey Park. He was often knocked by sportswriters for being a mediocre fielder, but when the chips were down he could be a real ball hawk. He didn't realize how serious the injury was, but through sheer grit and determination he remained in the game for eight full innings. Ted Williams was a superathlete who obviously had a very high threshold of pain."

Kiner's homer in the top of the ninth tied the score at 3-3 to send the game into extra innings.

◆

SLIDING HALL-OF-FAMER

MIKE "KING" KELLY of "Slide, Kelly, Slide" fame holds the distinction of compiling the worst fielding average of any member of baseball's Hall of Fame (elected 1945). In sixteen years in the majors (1876-93), mostly with Cincinnati, Chicago and Boston of the National League, he committed 753 errors out of 5,565 total chances, for an .865 percentage. And, Kelly, who saw service at every position, including pitching and catching, played in an era when fielders used very crude gloves or no gloves at all.

Kelly became a Hall of Famer, not for his fielding, of course, but because he was an excellent hitter (.313 average), a daring base-runner and a fierce competitor.

◆

BEWARE OF GROUND BALLS

BOBBY DOERR WAS BROUGHT UP to the majors with the Boston Red Sox in 1937—he was still only nineteen—and remained with the Bosox for fourteen seasons (skipping the 1945 campaign when he was in the U.S. Army), playing second base exclusively.

Named the American League's Most Valuable Player in 1944, he was picked for the A.L. All-Star Team.

Toward the end of the 1950 season and through 1951 Doerr began experiencing severe back pains. Though he was forced to miss fifty games in '51 because of those back problems, he still managed to hit .289, covered his position at second base, and was named for the eighth time to the All-Star team.

As the season progressed, however, the back pains grew worse, and there were times when he had difficulty putting on his suit coat after a game. Sometimes the trainer had to help him. Finally Doerr's doctors told him he'd have to quit playing altogether if he expected to remain in good health for the rest of his life.

Doerr made these comments on his problem: "Over the years I bent down so many thousands of times to pick up groundballs that my sacroiliac went out of whack. The doctors advised me in no uncertain terms that if I didn't stop playing I'd be walking around like a hunchback. I was only thirty-three, but, unfortunately, my playing career was finished."

Doerr was elected to the Hall of Fame in 1986.

◆

"SPECS"

"IF A FRAIL KID WITH A SLIGHT BUILD, weak eyes, and no high school or college training could jump directly from playing sand-lot baseball to the big leagues—and stick for seven seasons!—then almost any young player with a passion for the game can do the same thing.

"I was that kid I'm talking about. My baseball career started when one of my grammar school teachers (in New York City) organized a team of kids. I begged for a chance, but he ignored me because I wore thick glasses and I was small and skinny. No one had ever heard of wearing glasses when you played with a 'hard ball' in those days!

"But one day only eight players (and I) showed up. The teacher-manager had to use me in the outfield. I made a good catch and a couple of hits. From that day on, I was 'in.'"

SO BEGINS AN INSPIRING BOOK, *Baseball: From Back Yard to Big League,* by George "Specs" Toporcer, published in 1954 (Sterling), long after that incident in a gravel schoolyard on the East Side of New York City.

After starring for strong semi-pro teams in Brooklyn and New Jersey in 1919-20, Toporcer was noticed by major league scouts and signed a contract with the St. Louis Cardinals, then managed by Branch Rickey. He was invited to the Cards' spring training base at Orange, Texas and made the team as a second baseman. Thus, Specs Toporcer became the first player in the major leagues other than a pitcher to wear glasses on the field.

Toporcer wrote in his book: "Rickey sent me, skinny and bespectacled as I was, out onto the field in St. Louis to open the season for the Cardinals at second base! And to top it off, Rogers Hornsby, the league's leading hitter, was shifted to third to make room for me!"

Later in that 1921 season, the twenty-two-year-old Toporcer was farmed out to Syracuse, but he came back with the Cards in 1922 and stayed with them continuously through the first couple of weeks of the 1928 season when he was named player-captain of the Rochester Red Wings, the Cardinals' top farm club.

Toporcer's role in his seven seasons with St. Louis was mostly that of a utility infielder, with his best year being 1922 when he batted .324 in 116 games. In 1924 he hit a potent .313 in seventy games. Overall, in 546 big league games, he averaged .279 at the plate and was known as a sure-handed infielder.

He wrote further in his book: "During the seven years I was

with the Cardinals, I played next to Frankie Frisch, Grover Cleveland Alexander, Rogers Hornsby, Jim Bottomley, Billy Southworth, Chick Hafey, Ray Bales, 'Pop' Haines and many others. I had ample opportunity to study how they played the game."

Specs Toporcer really hit his stride as a player with the Red Wings as he was named the league's Most Valuable Player in 1929-30. In 1929, the pennant-winning Red Wings, with second baseman Toporcer as captain leading the way, reeled off 225 double plays, a mark that has never been eclipsed in organized baseball. The Red Wing infield, which was responsible for most of the twin killings, consisted of, in addition to Toporcer: "Rip" Collins, first base; Heinie Sand, shortstop; and Joe "Poison" Brown, third base.

Toporcer went from captain of the Red Wings to become a player-manager. In 1931, he went to Jersey City of the International League in that capacity, then back to Rochester, 1932-34. "Specs" last appeared in a regular season game as player-manager with Albany, New York, of the Class A Eastern League in 1941. One of his prize pupils at Albany in that year was an eighteen-year-old outfielder named Ralph Kiner, later to be the major league home run slugger and member of the Hall of Fame.

Specs remained in baseball as farm director of the Boston Red Sox and served his last stint as a minor league manager with Buffalo of the International League in 1951.

Tragically, after that 1951 season, Toporcer became completely blind, but he didn't allow anything to prevent him from being active in and around the baseball scene. Doctors had performed a major operation on his eyes, yet failed to save his sight. For a number of years he traveled the U.S.A. making speeches, primarily to young people.

"He'd tell them," recalled his wife Mabel (the Toporcers marked their sixty-sixth wedding anniversary in 1988), "that no matter what happens to you, don't give up." He never had a seeing-eye dog, and never needed a cane. "Mabel," he said, "has been my eyes."

Toporcer, who celebrated his ninetieth birthday on February 9, 1989, lived in Huntington Station, Long Island, N.Y., and still followed the game avidly through speaking with old friends from his baseball days and through radio broadcasts. When Specs Toporcer came onto the major league diamonds in 1920 wearing glasses, he made a real stir. Nowadays, however, no one gives a second thought to a player with "four eyes." Even Reggie Jackson wore glasses for most of his long career in the majors.

Maybe one of these days we'll see an umpire wearing glasses!

◆

TALES OF LEATHER

TWO CLASSIC STORIES STAND OUT when it comes to tales of defensive play.

First, a look at Dick Stuart, a notoriously poor-fielding first baseman. The man nicknamed Dr. Strangeglove was a Pirate fan favorite despite his shortcomings with the leather. Once day, a bat slipped out of the hands of an opposing batter. The bat whirled through the air towards first base, hit the turf, and then bounced all the way to Stuart. The first sacker came up with the bat cleanly, thus drawing good-natured cheers from a somewhat sarcastic crowd.

When asked if that was the most applause he'd ever heard, he responded, "No, one night thirty-thousand fans gave me a standing ovation when I caught a hot-dog wrapper on the fly."

Likewise, Johnny Mize could hit a ton, but was a leather liability at first base. When Mize was playing with the Giants for manager Leo Durocher, Mize also became the target of sarcasm. A fan mailed a letter to "Leo the Lip" which read: "Before each game an announcement is made that anyone interfering with or touching a batted ball will be ejected from the park. Please advise Mr. Mize that this doesn't apply to him."

◆

HUNG OUT TO DRY

JAY JOHNSTONE was a colorful character throughout his years in baseball. Although he was famous for his wild ways off the base-ball diamond, on the field he could be quite serious. For example, when he was playing right field for the Philadelphia Phillies he took part in a very unusual and tricky play.

Pittsburgh Pirates shortstop Frank Taveras was the runner at first base being held on by Dick Allen. The Pittsburgh hitter was their pitcher that day, Bruce Kison. It was an obvious bunt situa-tion, so when Kison squared around to bunt the ball, Taveras tried to get a healthy lead off first. Taveras noticed that the Phillis second baseman was shaded fairly far toward the second-base bag and that Allen was charging hard on each pitch in an effort to field the bun. Therefore, Taveras felt it was safe to try to get an even bigger lead.

He was too bold. When Kison did not bunt the next offering, catcher Johnny Oates saw Johnstone streak from his outfield posi-tion toward first base. Oates rifled the ball to Johnstone and Taveras was tagged out at first. Clearly, trick plays such as this can really pay off.

◆

HEADS UP!

AN EVENT TOOK PLACE on May 26, 1993, which will forever rank as one of the funniest and oddest plays ever. Cleveland's Carlos Martinez hit a ball deep to right where Texas Rangers outfielder Jose Canseco, hardly a Gold Glove fielder, was stationed.

From the very start, it was an adventure as Canseco misplayed the ball badly. He resembled a combination of a ballerina and a soccer player as he first pirouetted back on the ball before he "headed" it. That is to say, he actually had the ball bounce off his noggin and over the wall for perhaps the most bizarre home run ever.

Indians General Manager John Hart chuckled, "In my life I've never seen anything like that. I was stunned. I've seen balls hit outfielders on the head before, but not one that bounced over the fence."

Ace reliever Tom Henke later called the episode, "One of the funniest things I ever saw." Being a pitcher, he empathized with the pitcher who was victimized by this play, saying, "It wasn't funny for Kenny Rogers pitching at the time, but you still see that play over and over again, and it's still funny."

When reporters asked Texas infielder Julio Franco if he had ever seen such a play, his reply was: "Yeah, in a cartoon."

Cleveland's manager Mike Hargrove had a different viewpoint: "It amazes me he didn't go down. If a ball hit me that hard, I would have.

Canseco himself could only shake his infamous head and say laughingly, "Anybody got a bandage?"

◆

BASE RUNNING

4

THREE RUNNERS ON THIRD?
"DAFFY DODGERS" MANAGED IT

FLOYD CAVES HERMAN, a gangling six-foot-four-inch two-hundred-pound outfielder-first baseman, early in his career took on "Babe" as his nickname because as a powerful left-handed batter he reminded sportswriters and fans of Babe Ruth. After 5 years in the minors where he perfected his technique as a fence-buster who hit for a high average, Babe Herman, then twenty-three, was brought up to the majors in 1926 by the Brooklyn Dodgers.

From the early 1920s on, the Dodgers had ranked as a perennial second-division team under manager Wilbert Robinson, but they were a fun-loving bunch who became noted throughout baseball for being pranksters and practical jokers.

And Babe Herman, who had a wicked but delightful sense of humor, soon became the "Clown Prince" of the Dodgers, who came to be called the "Daffiness Boys." Herman was usually at the center of any zaniness involving the Dodgers and very quickly he established himself as a Brooklyn favorite for his penchant for being involved in the unusual and for his ability to hammer the ball. Unfortunately, he also gained the reputation of being a weak defensive outfielder and some fanciful stories were told about fly balls bouncing off his head.

The most bizarre of all incidents involving Babe Herman occurred in his rookie year, 1926, when he averaged a solid .319 and drove in eighty-one runs in 137 games. In a fateful mid-season game against the Boston Braves at Ebbets Field, Herman added the most unforgettable chapter to the Dodgers' history of bloopers.

With his pitcher, Dazzy Vance, on second and second baseman Chick Fewster on first with one out, Herman lined a shot to deep right-centerfield...the ball struck the bleacher wall, four-hundred feet from the plate, on the first bounce and bounded away. Vance, undecided whether the ball would be caught, hesitated between second and third. Fewster stopped after reaching second. Meanwhile, Herman, with his head down and his long legs churning, rounded first and raced for second. As the ball was hit safely, Fewster had no alternative but to take off for third, and force Vance to move on. Vance stood on the base as Fewster and Herman arrived there almost simultaneously. The ball by then had been relayed from the outfield to the second baseman, who rifled it to third. Fewster and Herman were tagged out. Vance was safe on the bag but died there. The side had been retired on what should have been a triple.

This, the weirdest double play in history, could have happened only in Brooklyn, it is said. However it didn't stop Babe Herman.

◆

HOW TO MAKE AN
UNASSISTED TRIPLE PLAY

THE UNASSISTED TRIPLE PLAY is one of the rarest plays in baseball, with only eight having occurred in the major leagues and only a handful in the minors.

But Walter Carlisle, a center-fielder for the Vernon team (in Los Angeles), on July 19, 1911, in a game against the Los Angeles Angels, executed perhaps the most spectacular unassisted triple play in professional baseball history.

With the score tied in the ninth inning, Charles Moore and George Metzger of the Angels walked. Pitcher Al Barson of Vernon was replaced by Harry Stewart. The Angels' third baseman, Roy Akin, connected on Stewart's first pitch for a low line drive over second base for what appeared to be a clean single. Moore from second and Metzger from first were off running on a hit-and-run signal. Carlisle, playing in close behind second, lunged forward and caught the liner just off the turf, ending with a somersault, landing on his feet (he had been a circus acrobat). He raced to second base and touched the bag, while Moore was well on his way to the plate; then he trotted to first, touching the bag to retire Metzger, who was still well past second.

Carlisle's name is secure in the record books since he is the only outfielder to have pulled off the unassisted triple play. (Tris Speaker, the Hall of Fame center-fielder active in the majors 1907-28, mostly with the Boston Red Sox and Cleveland, usually played in close and made several unassisted double plays, but never came close to running off the solo triple play.)

In recognition of Carlisle's singular achievement, the Vernon and Los Angeles fans presented him with a diamond-studded gold medal.

◆

RUNNING THE BASES BACKWARD

WHEN JIMMY PIERSALL, one of the most uninhibited spirits in baseball history, slammed out his one-hundreth major league homer while playing for the Washington Senators in 1963, he celebrated the occasion by running the bases backwards and sliding into home plate. Piersall probably thought at the time that this was going to be his last big home run—actually he managed to hit four more before he retired in 1967. Anyway, the league ruled that running the wrong way was illegal hereafter.

OPTICAL ILLUSION

DURING A 1969 CONTEST between the Atlanta Braves and the Houston Astros, a Houston base runner committed a terrible base blunder. His mistake was not due to disobeying a coach, being outwitted by an opponent, or being unaware of the game situation. Instead, his own faulty eyesight duped him.

It began with the runner taking a normal lead off third base. As the pitcher began his delivery, the runner danced down the baseline a few steps. Then, upon seeing the ball bounce wildly off the mitt of Atlanta catcher bob Didier, the daring runner darted home. It's hard to say who was more astonished a few seconds later, the runner or the catcher, but both were clearly perplexed. The runner couldn't believe his eyes because there was Didier, still squatting at the plate with the ball in his mitt. Didier, who had certainly not missed the ball, was wondering why the runner would dash for the well-guarded home plate. Didier, however, not so baffled that he didn't easily apply the tag for a ridiculously easy out.

The explanation? It turns out the runner had seen an object fly out of the catcher's glove. It seems Didier had been wearing a protective casing over a finger he had injured earlier. Since the casing was white, and since the impact of the ball meeting the mitt had caused it to soar toward the backstop, the runner had been deceived into thinking he could easily score. It was yet another odd and highly embarrassing baseball moment.

MORE HUMILIATION

MAX WEST WAS PLAYING for the Boston Red Sox when he perpetrated a strange faux pas. It started innocently enough when West was retired at first base on a routine groundout. On the play, a teammate advanced to third base. West trudged back to his dugout, and he apparently was extremely slow in doing so. As he was about to descend the steps and make his way to the bench, he spied a baseball.

He must have figured the ball had been fouled off by the next batter. So, as a friendly gesture, West stooped over, picked up the ball, and tossed it to the enemy catcher to save him a few steps.

But the ball had not been fouled off! It was in play, having escaped from the catcher after a pitch. In other words, it was a passed ball that would permit the runner off third to score. And, normally he would have scored with ease, but not when a teammate throws a perfect strike to the opposing catcher.

Needless to say, the runner was nailed at the plate. An official scorekeeper might even be tempted to teasingly give West an assist on the play. It's not quite certain what West's manager wanted to give him.

◆

HISTORY IN THE MAKING

BABE HERMAN WAS ONE OF baseball's zaniest players. His career, which spanned the years 1926-1945, is studded with odd plays. Most of those plays were due to his ineptitude. While he was a fine hitter (.324 lifetime), his attention to running and fielding skills was indifferent at best.

The most famous Herman tale has to be the time he hit a bases-loaded double which amazingly turned into a double play. To make matters worse, only one run scored on a play which should have probably, in fact, cleared the bases.

Herman's Brooklyn Dodgers were at the plate facing pitcher George Mogridge back on August 15, 1926, when he smacked a line drive off the right-field wall. Hank DeBerry scored easily from third base, of course. The runner on second, a pitcher named Dazzy Vance, advanced to third, but didn't run full speed for the plate. Perhaps because he was a pitcher he wasn't very skilled on the base paths and, therefore, made this base-running blunder. He decided he wouldn't succeed in making it home, so he scooted back to third instead.

Meanwhile, the Dodger on first base, Chick Fewster, having a different angle on the play, realized the ball was going to drop in for a base hit. He therefore made a dash for third. When he saw Vance retreat to third, Fewster slowed down between second and third so he could be able to trot back to second if Vance stayed put at third.

This comedy of errors reached its climax when Herman, running full tilt with his head down, tried to stretch his hit into a triple. At that point, Fewster had to continue to third base to prevent Herman from illegally passing him on the base path.

The end result was incredible—three men were all trying to occupy the same base! Eventually, two Dodgers were ruled out and Herman got credit for a double. In the process, he also gained instant baseball immortality for this remarkable gaff.

By the way, when the smoke cleared, it was Vance who was the only runner not declared out since he, as the lead runner, was entitled to stay at third. Only Fewster and Herman were ruled out. Hence, despite what some sources say, Herman did not triple into a triple play. Still, hitting a double that is turned into a double play is bad enough.

HISTORY REPEATING

IN 1997, HISTORY REPEATED ITSELF when Cleveland's Matt Williams doubled into a peculiar double play. When Williams strode to the plate, Jim Thome, who had drawn a walk, was on first with one out. Williams tattooed a pitch off Seattle's Bob Wolcott. The ball ricocheted off the left-field wall for what Williams knew was a sure double. Thome was chugging hard as he rounded third base.

At the last second, Thome's third-base coach thrust his hands up high, giving the signal for Thome to halt at third. Too late. The Mariners left fielder, Lee Tinsley, had quickly retrieved the ball and fired it back to the infield. Thome tried to scamper back to third, but was nailed as Russ Davis applied the tag.

In the meantime, Williams had seen Thome make the turn around third. Williams knew that if Thome raced for home plate the Mariners would throw the ball there and Williams could coast into third base. When the defense threw to third instead, Williams was trapped between second and third and was eventually tagged out after a rundown.

◆

KEEPING UP WITH THE JONESES

TWO WEIRD PLAYS occurred in two World Series separated by twelve years, but connected by one coincidence. During the 1957 series between the Milwaukee Braves and the New York Yankees, Nippy Jones appeared at the plate for the Braves. When he was hit on the foot by a pitch, he began to trot to first base as he was entitled to do.

However, the umpire didn't believe the ball had actually struck Jones. The ump felt the pitch had simply bounced off the dirt near home plate, so he ordered the batter back to the batter's box. Doing his best Perry Mason imitation, Jones retried Exhibit A, the ball, and showed a black smudge on the baseball. Convinced the mark was from the polish on Jones's shoe, the umpire finally awarded him first base.

Ironically, in the 1969 World Series involving the New York Mets and the Baltimore Orioles another player was hit on the foot. Once again, the batter claimed his right to go to first, and once more the umpire denied the claim.

Recalling the 1957 incident, the batter recreated the shoe polish scenario and won his plea, too. What makes this such an odds-defying event is the fact that the batter was also named Jones— Cleon in this case.

◆

BIZARRE BASE BURGLARY

CONTRARY TO A WIDELY HELD BELIEF, Herman "Germany" Schaefer was not the first man to "steal" first base. Still, his story is such a classic it is worth repeating as a sort of *Ripley's Believe-It-or-Not* play. In 1911, while playing for the Washington Senators, Schaefer was on first base while a teammate, Clyde Milan, was taking his lead off third. On the next pitch Schaefer took off for second, hoping to draw a throw from the catcher that might allow the runner from third to score. Instead of suc-ceeding on this double steal, Schaefer was able to take second unimpeded, since the catcher offered no throw.

Undaunted, on the next pitch Schaefer scampered back to first base, and was again ignored by the catcher. That was fine with Schaefer, known to be a "Clown Prince" of baseball. In this case, however, he had more in mind than just foolery.

His plan was to retreat to that base in order to set up the double steal again. Of course, he wasn't officially credited with a steal of first, but it's said that he did rattle the pitcher.

So, on the very next pitch Schaefer again streaked for second. For the second time in a matter of moments he stole that base. It's almost enough to lead to a facetious search of the record books for an entry, "most times stealing the same base during one at bat, twice by Schaefer, 1911."

What's more, the runner from third finally did cross home in one of the game's most peculiar plays ever. Needless to say, nowadays there is a rule forbidding such an event. The rulebook bans such tactics, as it makes a "travesty of the game."

◆

LARCENY IN HIS HEART

THERE ARE TIMES in baseball when a slow-footed runner gets a burst of inspiration and tries to steal a base. Thanks to a lumbering runner named Ping Bodie, there's even an ancient baseball saying regarding such instances. After Bodie was gunned out by a mile trying to steal, a writer penned the now famous words, "He had larceny in his heart, but lead in his feet."

Larry Parrish, like Bodie, had spikes of lead. During his career, which spanned nearly 1,900 major league games, the good-hit, no-run Parrish pilfered a mere thirty bases. In 1994, he was the manager of the Detroit Tigers AAA minor league team in Toledo. Parrish had his team running at every opportunity. By the end of the year, Toledo led the International League in steals. Parrish explained the rather anomalous situation by stating with a grin, "I always knew how to steal, I just couldn't do it."

◆

TRIPLE STEAL

JUST TO CLARIFY MATTES, as touched upon in "Bizarre Base Burglary," Herman "Germany" Schaefer was not the first man to "steal" first base. That man was Fred Tenney of the Boston Braves. Back on July 31, 1908, he was leading off first while Luther "Dummy" Taylor took his lead of a few steps off third. Cardinal pitcher Bugs Raymond was the pitcher, and Tenney stole second off him.

On the next pitch, Tenney (five weeks ahead of Schaefer) raced back to first base. With the next pitch he made yet another steal of second in an attempt to allow Taylor to score. Although this attempt didn't work, in a way Tenney pulled off a triple steal by himself!

◆

A MOVING "VIOLATION"

ONE MONTH PRIOR to the Seattle incident, Detroit's new manager Buddy Bell (in just his second game at the helm) did something no major-league skipper had ever done before. He gave the lumbering Cecil Fielder permission to steal base and got positive results! After a record 1,097-game dry spell, Fielder stole the first base of his career.

Second-base umpire Tim Tschida, tongue in cheek, observed that the accomplishment was "bigger than Nolan Ryan's seventh no-hitter."

Maybe so, after all, Ryan was capable of hurling a no-hitter virtually any time he took to the mound; Fielder at 250 (or more) pounds was never a threat to run. To rumble, perhaps, but not to run.

As for Fielder's reaction, he wanted to take the bag off the field immediately as a souvenir. He even joked with writers later saying, "I told you I was going to get one. I've been working hard on my jumps the last nine years. The pressure's off now. I'll go from here. Bell might start running me a little more."

After giving that idea a bit of thought, Fielder concluded, "I hope not." In fact, for the record, he ran just once more in 1996 and actually stole another base. At that point, he could proudly tease, "Two career steals and counting."

◆

CATCHING

5

MICKEY OWEN'S FAMOUS BLOOPER

BROOKLYN DODGERS catcher Mickey Owen entered the "Hall of Infamy" as the result of his play in Game 4 of the 1941 World Series (contested at Ebbetts Field) when he allowed a ball thrown by right-hander Hugh Casey for a third strike against the New York Yankees' Tommy Henrich to get past him for an error.

The Yankees, leading the Series two games to one, were in the process of losing Game 4 as the Dodgers carried a 4-3 lead going into the top of the ninth inning. Hugh Casey, the big Brooklyn right-hander, in his second relief role in two days, retired two Yankees to start the inning. Victory seemed to be at hand for the Dodgers as Henrich came up to the plate. With the count one ball and two strikes, Casey threw a sweeping curve, missing the plate by more than a foot. Henrich swung at it, however, and that strikeout should have ended the inning and the game. BUT hold on! Catcher Mickey let the third strike get away from him. Henrich, on the alert, dashed off and reached first safely as the ball rolled toward the backstop.

What happened next is "history." Joe DiMaggio, always tough in the clutch, followed with a single and Charlie Keller proceeded to line a two-run double which put the Yankees ahead. After Bill Dickey walked, Joe Gordon added insult to injury when he also smashed a two-run double to run the score to 7-4.

Yankee reliever "fireman" Johnny Murphy, who had entered the game in the eighth, retired the Dodgers in order in the bottom of the ninth to send Dodger fans home in misery, two games behind.

In Game 5, Ernie "Tiny" Bonham threw a four-hitter at the Dodgers in a 3-1 victory that clinched the Series, four games to one.

The Yankees had now won their 8th straight world Series, a strait "Fall Classic," a streak dating back to 1916.

Mickey Owen was obviously the "goat" of the Series, but did he really deserve that odious label? Not according to Tommy Henrich himself. One of the authors of this book interviewed Henrich at length during the course of a January 28, 1989, baseball memorabilia show in New York where "Old Reliable," as he came to be called, appeared as a guest. Henrich acknowledged: "Owen really didn't have much of a chance to stop that ball. Hugh Casey somehow managed to throw a wide sweeping curve—one of the biggest 'benders' I ever saw in my life—that suddenly broke down and hit at least a foot in front of the plate. The pitch fooled me completely, and it, or course, fooled Owen as well. Even an octopus would have had a helluva time getting a glove on that ball. Owen was really a victim of circumstances and undeservedly got a bad rap."

How did Mickey Owen view that unfortunate play of nearly a half-century ago? Observed Owen: "I played pro ball for more than twenty years and considered myself a pretty fair country catcher. My record proves it. That third strike curve from Hugh Casey was really a dandy, and if the ball had carried twenty-four inches or so further, I would have caught it easily. As it is, that one play made me famous, and even to this day I get more invitations for paid appearances than I have time for. Who said 'Life isn't fair'?"

◆

THE CATCHING SHORTSTOP-MANAGER

LOU BOUDREAU, an extremely versatile athlete, played both varsity basketball and baseball for the University of Illinois in 1936-38. In fact, he was better known as a basketball star than as a ballplayer during his collegiate days, scintillating as both a guard and forward on Illinois' famed "Whiz Kids" five of the period.

When Boudreau was called up by the Cleveland Indians in mid-season 1939 from Buffalo of the International League, he was already regarded as one of the best fielding shortstops in the game, with his sensational play. He starred for Cleveland immediately at the vital infield spot, captivating fans all over the American League.

When the managership of the Indians opened up in 1942, team owner Alva Bradley at first didn't even think of tapping Boudreau for the post until Lou made formal application. "Who can do the job better than me?" Boudreau remarked after he was hired. Boudreau, a born leader, was only twenty-four at the time, the youngest pilot ever in major league history. (Boudreau held forth as the Indians' player-manager for nine full seasons before moving on to the Boston Red Sox, first as a player, then as a manager.)

In the sweltering heat of an August 1943 Sunday double-header at Cleveland's Municipal Stadium, both of Boudreau's two regular catchers, Buddy Rosar and Gene Desautels, were knocked out with injuries by the fifth inning of the second game. No other catchers were available on the entire Indians roster. What to do?

Without hesitating for a moment, manager Boudreau himself donned the catcher's gear and handled the backstop position flaw-lessly for the next four innings. "I wouldn't ask any of my players to do what I couldn't do myself," Boudreau told reporters after the game.

"But you never caught a game in pro ball before today," injected a writer from the *Cleveland Press*.

"A real ballplayer can play *any* position!" Boudreau shot back.

Boudreau injected himself as an emergency backstop on two other occasions, once in 1944 and once again in 1948, the latter being the Indians' World Championship year.

In that glorious 1948 season for the Indians, Lou Boudreau, the "Flaming Frenchman," earned the distinction of becoming the first and only player-manager to win the MVP award.

The Indians and the Boston Red Sox ended the regular season in a dead heat with records of 96-58, but in a dramatic one-game playoff—the first in American League history—Boudreau paced his mates to an 8-3 victory with a 4-for-4 performance that included two homers.

For the 1948 season, Boudreau batted a robust .355 (second only to Ted Williams's .369) as he rapped out 199 hits, scored 116 runs, and drove in 106. Incredibly, he walked ninety-eight times and struck out on only nine occasions in '48.

◆

A STRANGE BREED

WHEN A PLAYER DONS the "tools of ignorance" and takes a stand behind the plate, he knows he's taking a risk of getting his fingers broken and his legs and feet bruised, not once but many times.

Al Lopez was brave enough to set the world record of 1,918 games behind the plate in his twenty years in baseball, 1928-47.

Interestingly, when Al Lopez was managing the Indians in the 1950s, one of his star players, 1951 to 1953, was a hard-hitting short-stop-third baseman named Ray Boone. Papa Boone used to bring his little son, Bob, always dressed up in a baseball uniform to the game and let him work out on the sidelines.

Lopez may have given the younger Boone some tips on catching at the time or just set a fine example, but little did he know that this tot would eventually break Lopez's own endurance record for catchers.

And when he got his chance, that is exactly what Bob did.

Bob Boone (born November 19, 1947) accomplished the feat in a relatively short time period, fewer than fifteen full major league seasons. After spending nearly five years in the minor leagues, he broke in with the Philadelphia Phillies in the latter part of the 1972 campaign, became their regular catcher the next year, and nine years later was traded to the Angels at the beginning of 1982.

Along the way he also played a few games in the outfield and at third and first base, but those don't count toward the record, of course.

At the conclusion of his record-breaking game, Boone, the new "King of Squat," commented: "The record means I've taken more aspirin and other forms of painkillers than another player in history." Then he added the obligatory "I play baseball to help my team win, not for personal goals or records."

The Hall of Fame in Cooperstown requested Boone's glove for display, but he rugged backstop's reply was "No, I've still got some games to catch with it."

ANOTHER CATCHER, JOHN BATEMAN, a hulking six-foot-three-inch 225-pounder, hit eighty-one home runs in a ten-year big league career with the Houston Astros, Montreal Expos, and Philadelphia Phillies from 1963 to 1972, and wound up as a softball star. A righthanded hitter with pretty fair power, Bateman required 1,017 games in baseball to knock out those eighty-one homers.

After Bateman was released by the Phillies early in 1973, he had to be content to play with the Houston Bombers softball team for the next several years. One day toward the end of 1976 Eddie Feigner saw Bateman smash a mammoth 450-foot softball homer at the Houston Astrodome.

Feigner went to Bateman and promptly signed him up for his "The King and His Court," a four-man softball team. Feigner was such a great softball pitcher that he required only three "back-up" men on his team (a shortstop, a first baseman, and a catcher) to contend on even terms against a regular ten-player softball team.

Bateman fit in well with Feigner and his "Court," and in his first full season in top-level fast-pitch softball in 1978 he connected for 179 homers and 221 games. In one game, he hit five. At season's end Bateman chortled: "Who needs the big leagues? With 'The King and His Court' I hit for a better average, drive out more homers, and play on a winner. In fact, I make better money playing softball then I did hardball."

◆

THE HIDDEN POTATO TRICK

THE SELECTION HERE for the greatest trick of all time is a sort of variation on the hidden ball trick. It took place on August 31, 1987, during a meaningless minor league contest. Dave Bresnahan, Williamsport's catcher, and the great-nephew of one of the greatest catchers of all time, Roger Bresnahan, devised a fantastic and unconventional scheme.

He knew the time was right to unveil his plan when a runner from the opposing Reading team had raced home, and another runner, Rick Lundblade, pulled up at third. Bresnahan had been waiting for just such a situation.

So, Bresnahan asked the home plate umpire for a time-out, saying he needed a new mitt. What the runner on third did not realize was that the new glove had a peeled potato hidden inside. As the next pitch came in to Bresnahan, he held the potato in his bare hand. He then intentionally threw the vegetable wildly, like a hot potato, past third and into the outfield.

Lundblade saw the white blur streak by and assumed it was the ball being thrown on a pickoff attempt—after all, how many potatoes does a guy see whizzing around a baseball diamond! So, at that point he naturally headed to the plate.

Bresnahan, of course, was waiting there for him, ball in hand. It was a sort of "Now you see it, now you see it again" bit of prestidigitation.

However, the ump ruled Lundblade safe, calling the play a balk (or an error, depending on which version is being told of this tale). Not only that, the creative catcher was later: 1) ejected from the game, 2) fined $50 by the Williamsport manager, Orlando Gomez, 3) labeled "unprofessional," and 4) was even released from the team by the Cleveland Indians, the "parent" major league club of the Williamsport Bills (of course, the catcher's .149 average at the time didn't help his cause any).

Ironically, two nights later this seventh-place team ran a promotion for its last game of the year. Any fan bringing a potato to the game got in for one dollar. Bresnahan even returned to the park and autographed potatoes with the inscription, "This spud's for you."

He also made appearances on David Letterman's television show and on an NBC pre-game show. He once joked of his fame, "I could run for governor of Idaho."

In 1988, he again visited Bowman Field, the site of his infamy, where the team now honored him by painting his uniform number on the outfield fence. A team spokesperson quipped, "He's probably the only .149 hitter to ever have his jersey retired."

As if to prove the cliché, "There's nothing new under the sun," it should be noted that the same potato play had already been performed a few years earlier by a high-school team. In fact, the coach in this case had actually practiced the play with his kids.

◆

CATCH 'EM IF YOU CAN

ANOTHER CATCHER, Sandy Alomar of the Indians, came up with his own trick a few years ago. Mike Felder of the Mariners was on first base with one out. As Cleveland's pitcher Charles Nagy fired a ball to the plate, Felder took off for second. He had such a fine jump, Alomar sensed no throw would be good enough to nail the base thief. So, using guile, Alomar intentionally lobbed the ball in a very high trajectory over the infield. He made his throw appear to be a pop-up.

Fans thought the ball had merely slipped out of the catcher's grasp. The truth was he aimed the ball to second basement Carlos Baerga, hoping Felder would see the ball high in the air and be fooled into thinking a Seattle teammate had hit a pop fly.

If it worked, Felder would scurry back to first or perhaps hesitate enough to even become a victim of a most unusual "caught stealing." Baseball accounts reveal this scam didn't work, but Alomar was using his head by coming up with yet another creative trick play.

◆

THOU SHALL NOT WALK

IN 1995 ANOTHER INDIAN CATCHER, Tony Pena, helped engineer a replication of a very famous decoy. California's Chili Davis was in the batter's box facing veteran right-hander Dennis Martinez.

The count was full, at three balls and two strikes, with a runner on third.

Pena crouched behind the plate for the payoff pitch, and then suddenly stood and signaled for an intentional walk.

Seeing he was about to be given a free pass to first, Davis relaxed. And at that moment, Martinez quickly slipped strike three by Davis. The irate batter later stated, "I got suckered. I've never seen it before and I'll never see it again."

Well, if he was watching baseball highlights a year later, he certainly did see that play executed again. On July 30, 1996, Pena, who said he performed this play once with Roger Clemens in Boston and several more times in winter ball, did it once more. This time, the victim was John Olerud, then with the Toronto Blue Jays. Martinez and Pena again worked the con game to perfection on a two-out payoff delivery.

Olerud contended he wasn't fooled as two of his coaches had yelled a warning. "Martinez made a great pitch down and away," claimed Olerud. "It might have looked like I was tricked, but I wasn't."

At any rate, the ironic part of it all is the fact that this trick is extremely famous. When Chili Davis, Tony Pena's victim in 1995, was twelve years old, the Oakland A's pulled it off during the 1972 World Series. It's almost as if Davis (and Olerud?) were proving the axiom that those who don't learn from events of the past are doomed to repeat such errors.

THE WORLD SERIES DECEPTION OF 1972 took place in the fifth inning of the fifth game. The A's superlative reliever Rollie Fingers was on the mound, trying to help his team cling to 4-3 lead over Cincinnati. Fingers was clearly in a jam as the Reds had Bobby Tolan leading off first base with the highly feared Johnny Bench at the plate. A few moments later, Tolan swiped second as the count reached two balls and two strikes.

It was then that the Oakland skipper, Dick Williams, went to the mound for a conference. As he strolled off the field, he pointed to first base and said, "Okay, let's put him on." Needless to say, Bench fell for it—after all, the situation obviously did call for an intentional walk. The bat lay on his shoulders as Rollie Fingers slipped a third strike past him.

Seconds later, a job well done, Fingers and his catcher Gene Tenace were jogging to the dugout as Bench stared at the plate in sheer disbelief, a strikeout casualty.

◆

THE GUYS IN CHARGE

6

UMPING OUTFIELDER

O N A HOT SUMMER afternoon late in the 1935 season during a Chicago White Sox-St. Louis Browns game at Sportsman's Park, St. Louis, home plate umpire E. T. "Red" Ormsby was overcome by the heat. No other umpire was available or on the field. What to do? John Bertrand "Jocko" Conlan, a White Sox outfielder was a veteran who knew the rules. So he was asked to fill in on an emergency basis! Conlan, still wearing his White Sox uniform, was glad to oblige, and umpired the rest of the game. Everyone at the park was impressed with the fact that Jocko made his calls fair and square in every instance. It was the start of a brilliant umpiring career for Jocko.

"You'd never see an incident like this happen today, recalled Conlan recently. "A player in uniform calling a major league game? Baseball was a little more informal back then."

Conlan, thirty-six at the time he made his "debut" as an arbiter, had already spent sixteen years as a player in the majors and minors, but decided right then and there that umpiring was for him. His formal apprenticeship calling balls and strikes began in 1936 in the Class A New York-Pennsylvania League. After two years in that circuit, he moved up to the American Association, and after three years of additional seasoning in the A. A. was promoted to the National League in 1941.

Conlan, for the next twenty-four years, ranked as one of the top umps in the game.

Jocko Conlan credits Bill Klem, "The Old Arbitrator," for promoting him to the majors. Klem, a National League umpire for thirty-six years (1905-40), was chief of N.L. staff after his retirement from the field and personally selected all new recruits.

"Klem taught me to never back away from a player, especially around the home plate area. Home plate is the umpire's domain and he's got to protect it," declared Conlan.

Klem in 1953 became the first umpire to gain election to baseball's Hall of Fame in Cooperstown.

Both Klem and Conlan had nemeses from the managerial ranks who gave them real trouble over the year. Klem's chief tormentor was New York Giants manager John McGraw, while Conlan had a long string of memorable confrontations with Leo Durocher. Once, during a particularly heated argument, Durocher kicked dirt on Conlan and Jocko returned the insult by kicking dirt right back at Lippy Leo.

Conlan retired from the field after the 1964 season at the age of sixty-five, and even while in his sixties he was known for his zip and aggressiveness.

In 1974, Jocko Conlan won election to the Hall of Fame, an honor given only to six umpires in the 115-year history of the major leagues. (In addition to Klem, the others are Tom Connolly, Billy Evans, Cal Hubbard, and Al Barlick.)

Bill Guilfoile, editor of the *Baseball Hall of Fame & Museum Yearbook*, has written of Conlan: "A polka-dot bow tie, a balloon chest protector, and quick grin became his trademarks; and he won the respect of the players and fans alike with his hustle, accuracy and fairness."

As he approached his ninetieth birthday in 1988, Jocko retained his fierce enthusiasm for the diamond game and appeared regularly at baseball card shows and conventions all across the United States. On a good weekend Conlan was known to give out his autograph two-thousand and more times. He'd sign anything.

"I've finally figured out a way to make a little bit of money out of baseball," quipped Jocko.

HAZARDOUS IN JAPAN

UMPIRING IN THE ASIAN big leagues is perhaps what American baseball men criticize most sharply. If you think umpires take a lot of flack in America, you should see what they go through in Japan.

"Umpires in Japan don't really control the game as tightly as umpires do in the States, and there's a great deal of trouble as a consequence," observed Jim Lefebvre, who played for Tokyo's Lotte Orions in the 1970s, and who is now managing the Seattle Mariners.

In the U.S. umpires rarely change their decisions. In Japan they frequently do, sometimes two or three times before holding fast.

George Altman, a National League outfielder in the 1960s, who went on to play for the Lotte Orions for nearly a decade, recalls one game that was held up for more than an hour while the umpires debated whether an Orion batter had interfered with an opposing player trying to reach first base. The umpires kept switching their ruling, depending on which manager was arguing loudest and strongest. The debate ended only after the Orions' manager finally acceded to the umpires' fervent pleas that he allow his batter to be called out.

A second base umpire changed his ruling twice before a packed house at Tokyo's Korakuen Stadium and the resultant bitter dispute delayed the game for nearly forty-five minutes. "If umpires in Japan would only learn to stand their ground after making calls on close plays, there would be a lot less trouble all around," observed Jim Hicks, a veteran of both the U.S. and Japanese big leagues.

All too frequently, umpires are physically attacked by players in Japan. "Thumping the ump" has been an almost regular occurrence. In the U.S., a player could be suspended for the season or barred from baseball for life for attacking an umpire, but in Japan the offender usually draws a light fine or a brief suspension.

George Altman particularly remembers one game when he was filling in temporarily at first base for the Orions; he registered a mild protest after the umpires had called a batter safe and Altman thought he was out. "Before I could say more than a couple of words, our second baseman came over and shoved the ump about three or four feet. Then the catcher, shortstop, and right-fielder arrived, and someone really unloaded, knocking the ump to the ground," Altman said.

"The ump was only a little guy, added Altman. "and I was beginning to feel sorry for him when our manager finally arrived from the dugout. I thought he would break up the skirmish, but he started shoving the umpire with the rest of the bunch!"

Joe Lutz, a veteran of more than twenty years in U.S. organized baseball, in 1975 became the first American to manage a Japanese team when he took the reins of the Hiroshima Toyo Carp in the Central League. Lutz, who had gained the respect of the Japanese baseball establishment, seemed on his way toward a long tenure as the Carp's manager, but he didn't last half the season.

It seemed that during a game in June, there was a close play at the plate and the umpire changed his decision *three times* before making a final call to the disfavor of the Carp. Lutz quit his job right on the spot and grabbed a plane back to the U.S. the very next day, never to return.

Mercifully, it appears that in recent years the Japanese have been sending better-trained umpires out onto the field.

◆

EJECTED

THE ARGUMENTATIVE Bobby Valentine, who managed the Texas Rangers since 1985, had been ejected seventeen times in his career for arguing—by seventeen different umpires. Valentine certainly doesn't believe in playing favorites.

◆

THE TEARS OF AN UMPIRE

GAME 5 OF THE 1956 WORLD SERIES between the New York Yankees and Brooklyn Dodgers, longtime arch rivals, drew a near sell-out crowd of 64,519 fans at Yankee Stadium. The Series was knotted at two games each and the Yankees were anxious to atone for their loss in the 1955 post-season classic to the Dodgers.

Don Larsen, one of the victims in the Yankees' loss in Game 2, took the mound against the Dodgers' Sal Maglie. Larsen, a big six-foot-four-inch right-hander, had gotten himself into the Yankee doghouse in spring training in Florida when he rammed his car into a tree after a late-evening bar-hopping session. Larsen redeemed himself over the course of the season by posting an 11-5 mark as a spot starter.

The home plate umpire for this crucial game was Ralph "Babe" Pinelli, sixty-one years old; after the Series' conclusion he was scheduled to retire as a National League arbiter following two decades of service. Before he took up calling balls and strikes, Pinelli had been a professional ballplayer for fifteen years, spending eight seasons in the majors as an infielder.

The fans at Yankee Stadium began going into a frenzy, for they realized that through eight innings Larsen had allowed neither a hit nor a runner to reach first base. Now in the ninth he retired the first batter, Carl Furillo, on a fly ball to right. After Roy Campanella grounded out to second, Manager Walter Alston sent his best pinch hitter, left-handed Dale Mitchell to bat for pitcher Maglie. Then with the count one ball and two strikes, Mitchell took a called third strike as the Stadium exploded with a deafening roar.

Don Larsen had become the first pitcher in the fifty-three-year history of the World Series to throw a no-hitter.

Larsen and the Yankees were happy, but Babe Pinelli was extremely disappointed. Not one of the Yankee players, nor the manager, nor coaches, nor Larsen, had come up to him after the game to thank him for his perfect performance. Later, Pinelli broke down and cried. He said, "Hell, there was a lot of pressure on Larsen, but look at the pressure there was on me. I had to call the balls and strikes! Just look back...neither of the teams put up an argument over my calls at any time during the game. Umpires never get the credit they deserve."

This was also Dale Mitchell's final game as a big leaguer, after an eleven-year career in the majors, spent mostly with Cleveland. Mitchell, a .312 lifetime hitter, never argued the called third strike because he knew the pitch was within the strike zone. Mitchell commented later: "Here I average better than .300 for a career, get more than two-hundred hits in a season twice, play on three pennant winners, and all people remember me for now is that I took a called third strike to give Don Larsen his perfect game in the World Series."

◆

CONSERVING ENERGY

BACK A COUPLE OF GENERATIONS ago, major league baseball was conducted on a less formal basis than nowadays and Henry Emmett ("Heinie") Manush, a hard-hitting outfielder, seemed to exemplify that laid-back style.

Toward the mid-1930s, Manush, already a grizzled veteran then wearing the uniform of the Washington Senators (he had broken into the majors with Detroit in 1923 and won the A.L. batting crown as a Tiger in 1926 with a fat .378 mark) made it a point of conserving his energy during the "dog days" of summer.

For example, whenever the Senators rolled into Cleveland to play the Indians at League park, Manush, a leftfielder, found a way of saving hundreds of steps each game.

After the Indians would finish in their half of an inning at bat, if Manush wasn't scheduled to bat in the Senators' half—unless there was a rally—he never walked from his left-field post back to the visitors' third base dugout. He simply walked over to the left-field bleachers directly in back of him, opened a little wire gate, sat himself down on a wooden bench and relaxed in the company of ticket-paying fans until the Indians were ready to bat again, and he had to resume his position in the outfield.

"Why the hell should I walk two-hundred-some feet to the dugout when the bleachers are right in back of me?" Manush once told a reporter.

Manush's "energy conservation" tactics paid off handsomely because he lasted twenty-five years as a professional player (seventeen seasons in the majors, lifetime batting average .330) and gained election to baseball's Hall of Fame in 1964.

◆

WALTER ALSTON, HOME RUN SLUGGER

YOU KNOW that Walter Alston, long-time manager of the Dodgers, played in only one game in the major leagues and had a single at-bat. (He struck out.) But did you know he was a power hitter in the Middle Atlantic League with a total of 176 circuit clouts, leading the league in homers no than four times?

◆

MENTAL LAPSE

A COLLEGE PROFESSOR can be excused for being absentminded, but not a big league umpire during the course of a ball game. Because Vic Delmore became absentminded at a St. Louis Cardinals-Chicago Cubs game played at Wrigley Field on June 30, 1959, he caused one of the strangest and most bizarre plays in baseball history.

The Cards' top hitter Stan Musial was at bat with a 3-1 count when the next pitch got away from Cub catcher Sammy Taylor and skidded toward the backstop.

Umpire Delmore called "ball four" and Musial trotted toward first. But Taylor and pitcher Bob Anderson argued vehemently with the ump that it was a foul tip.

Since the ball was still in play, and Taylor had not chased it, Musial ran toward second. Fast-thinking third baseman Alvin Dark then raced to the backstop and retrieved the ball. Meanwhile, Delmore was still involved in the argument with the Cub battery mates when he unthinkingly pulled a second ball out of his pocket and handed it to catcher Taylor. Suddenly noticing Musial dashing for second, pitcher Anderson grabbed the new ball and threw to second—at the same time that Dark threw to short-stop Ernie Banks with the original ball!

Anderson's throw sailed over second base into center-field. Musial saw the ball fly past his head, so—not realizing there were two balls in play—he took off for third only to run smack into Banks who tagged him out with the original ball.

After a lengthy conference, the umpires ruled that Musial was out since he was tagged with the original ball.

Also called "out" was Vic Delmore himself. Citing a "lack of confidence" in Vic, National League President Warren Giles fired him at season's end.

◆

DR. JEKYLL AND MR. HYDE

IN 1886, ROBERT LOUIS STEVENSON published one of his best known stories, *The Strange Case of Dr. Jekyll and Mr. Hyde*. In this horror-fantasy, Stevenson spins tale of a man with a dual personality: Dr. Jekyll, the brilliant physician, is able to periodically transform himself into the viciously criminal Mr. Hyde. Of all the major figures in baseball today, George M. Steinbrenner III stands as, perhaps, the most controversial because of his obvious dual personality.

On one hand, Steinbrenner is able to perform extremely magnanimous deeds, and on the other he does many perfectly awful things.

Before Steinbrenner became principal owner of the New York Yankees in 1973, he owned the Cleveland Pipers professional basketball team which nearly went bankrupt, and from that point he was anxious to gain control of a major sports franchise so that he could turn it into a success. His fortune is based on his ownership of the American Shipbuilding Co., now based in Tampa, Florida. Here we'll offer a brief representative list of five "Mr. Hydes for Steinbrenner and five "Dr. Jekylls."

MR. HYDE:

(1) Shortly after he gained control of the Yankees, Steinbrenner showed a definite lack of knowledge of many facets of baseball. In spring training in Florida, for example, he ordered one of his players to wear his cap properly. The player did have his cap on backwards, but he was a catcher!

(2) Shows an extreme lack of tolerance for a player making an error. Once when Bobby Murcer muffed an outfield ground ball in a spring exhibition game, Steinbrenner blurted: "I'm paying him more than $100,000 a year and he can't catch the ball."

(3) Seems to take sadistic pleasure in squashing little people. Once he had the switchboard operator in a Boston hotel fired because she wouldn't allow him to place a long-distance call from the telephone in a bar, as per regulations.

(4) Constantly ridicules his top players in public. He has, for example, called Dave Winfield "Mr. May" for ostensibly not performing well in late season stretch drives—and even criticized Don Mattingly for being "selfish" after he hit a record-tying eight homers in eight straight games in 1987. Mattingly injured his wrist shortly after this record string, and Steinbrenner blamed it on Mattingly's "exaggerated home run swing."

(5) Whenever the Yankees begin playing badly, Steinbrenner pushes the panic button and starts firing, or threatening to fire, his managers and pitching coaches. Steinbrenner changed managers at least 14 times since 1973, and has had an uncounted number of pitching coaches. In 1982, when the Yankees finished a dismal fifth

in the Eastern Division, Steinbrenner employed three different managers during the season: Bob Lemon, Gene Michael, and Clyde King. Before Steinbrenner fires a manager, he usually embarrasses him no end in the public press.

DR. JEKYLL:

(1) Steinbrenner may fire his managers as often as some people change their socks, but he ordinarily doesn't kick them out of the Yankees organization. They remain on the payroll either as general manager, super-scout, special assistant, or coach, if they so desire—and at handsome salaries. Ex-Yankee managers who've stayed on with the organization in one capacity or another include: Lou Piniella, Bob Lemon, Gene Michael, Clyde King, and of course, Billy Martin.

(2) In 1979, Steinbrenner led a delegation down to Curacao in the Caribbean in order to assist the Curacao Baseball Federation, both with special instruction and a generous donation of baseball equipment. Yogi Berra and Billy Martin, among others, accompanied Steinbrenner on this little publicized goodwill tour.

(3) Reggie Jackson helped Steinbrenner achieve some of his greatest successes during Reggie's five years with the Yankees—but was let go after 1981 because he was thought to be "over-the-hill." However, after Jackson hit his fifth major league homer with the California angels in 1984, Steinbrenner presented him with a very expensive sterling silver platter commemorating the event.

(4) Steinbrenner made it a point to make a special trip to Cooperstown in July 1987 to witness Jim "Catfish" Hunter's induction into baseball's Hall of Fame. Steinbrenner signed Hunter as his first major free agent in 1975, and Catfish responded by playing a major role in helping the Yankees capture three American League pennants. No one appreciates true achievement more than George.

(5) George M. Steinbrenner appreciates true achievement in any field. For example, he long admired the work of George E. Seedhouse, Supervisor of Community Centers and Playgrounds in Cleveland, Ohio, during the 1950s and 1960s. and in recognition of that work he named one of his American shipbuilding Col. Iron ore carriers (a thirteen-thousand-ton vessel) *George E. Seedhouse.*

◆

SHOWMAN EXTRAORDINAIRE

WHEN BILL VEECK (as in "wreck") bought the Cleveland Indians in 1946, he took over a moribund baseball franchise that hadn't fielded a pennant winner since 1920. With an incredible flair for showmanship, he succeeded in boosting the season's attendance to over 1,050,000, shattering all previous Indians' records, though the team never managed to climb out of sixth place that year.

Veeck believed that when fans came to the ball park they should be entertained totally. For starters, he hired several jazz combos to wander through the stands and perform at the end of each half-inning.

Next he hired former minor league pitcher Max Patkin, a contortionist, to coach occasional innings at third base. One of the strangest-looking characters ever to wear a baseball uniform, Patkin made it difficult for opposing pitchers to concentrate on the game as they couldn't help watching Max twist himself in and out of pretzel shapes along the coaching lines. Coaches rarely receive applause of any kind, but the fans howled with glee at the sight of "Coach" Patkin, and sometimes gave him standing ovations for his outlandish performances.

At about the time Patkin became an Indian, Veeck signed up thirty-three-year-old minor league infielder and stuntman Jackie Price as a player-coach. Price pulled off feats never seen before on a ball field. Among other things, he could throw two or three balls simultaneously and make them all curve, he could catch balls dropped from blimps high in the air and even play an occasional game of shortstop for Cleveland.

One of Jackie's most memorable stunts was to suspend himself upside down from a twelve-foot-high horizontal bar, grab a bat and have balls pitched to him which he hit distances of 150 feet and more. Fans jammed their way into the park to watch Patkin and Price go through their extraordinary acts.

BILL VEECK HAD OPERATED the Milwaukee Brewers of the American Association with great success in the early 1940s and in recognition of his achievements he was named in 1942 by *The Sporting News* as minor league executive of the year. He was only twenty-eight then. Shortly after his Milwaukee Brewers exploits, Veeck entered the U.S. Marine Corps, was shipped off to the South Pacific, and while stationed at Bougainville during the height of World War II, sustained a severe injury to his right leg as the result of an artillery training exercise. Unfortunately, the leg never healed properly, but during that hectic summer of '46 Veeck hobbled around through the grandstands daily, talking to the fans and getting their views as to how the Indians could be improved. Numerous times after an arduous day promoting the team, Veeck would write in pain at night as his leg flared up.

Infection set in and on November 1, 1946, the leg was amputated nine inches below the knee. Shortly after the operation, Veeck, still under the influence of anesthesia and quite woozy, grabbed the telephone and called Franklin Lewis, sports editor of the *Cleveland Press*, to see how the Indians came out in the major league draft. Baseball was always on his mind.

Veeck was fitted with an artificial leg, but the pain did not disappear, and there were other operations until finally in 1961 he had to have amputation above the knee. During all those years he never permitted physical pain to dim his enthusiasm for baseball. On frequent occasions he removed the artificial leg and amused friends by using it as an ashtray.

"Wild Bill," as he was called by the local writers, used every sort of promotion imaginable. One night, for example, he would give the ladies orchids specially flown in from Hawaii, and on another night he would have former Olympic track champion Jesse Owens dress up in an Indians uniform and run a footrace against one of his players. Owens, then well into his thirties, generally won.

Unpredictable "Wild Bill" suddenly sold the team (at an enormous profit) and took a year's sabbatical from baseball before he bought the St. Louis Browns in 1951. Veeck used more promotional gimmicks to draw fans into Sportsman's Park to watch his inept Browns in action: He gave away a two-hundred-pound block of ice one night, and another time live lobsters, and in desperation he sent a midget up to the plate to pinch-hit.

Bill surfaced again when he bought the Chicago White Sox at the end of 1958. He reached his peak as a master showman when he introduced the exploding scoreboard at Chicago's Comiskey Park. Every time a White Sox player hit a homer the scoreboard would erupt into a crescendo of sound and shoot off a fireworks rocket display. Other major league owners were shocked and called it an "outrage," but the fans loved it. Eventually other teams in both leagues installed their own exploding scoreboards.

Veeck was forced to sell the Sox after the 1961 season because of a severe illness. He reemerged as a big league owner for the fourth and last time in 1975, when he headed a group that again bought the financially ailing White Sox. Next, "Wild Bill" had his team wear short pants during the hot days of summer in 1976. One sportswriter fumed. "The White Sox look like an amateur softball team." However, Veeck at no time allowed his critics to hamper his highly individualistic style of running baseball teams. He spent some of his last years rooting in the bleachers, sitting bare-chested and chatting with the other fans.

◆

LEAVING THE BENCH FOR A TASTY TREAT

WHEN LUKE APPLING was managing the Kansas City Athletics on an interim basis late in the 1967 season, he became so bored with the game that he went up behind the grandstand and ordered a hot dog and beer from a refreshment stand. He didn't come back down into the dugout until he had finished his repast. Result: Appling, an easygoing southerner, was not invited to manage the Athletics for the 1968 season.

Appling, the Hall of Fame shortstop, who played twenty years for the Chicago White Sox (1930-50), remained in various coaching capacities, however, after his Kansas City experience. He made baseball headlines in 1985 when at the age of seventy-eight he slammed a home run into the left-field stands at Washington, D.C.'s Robert F. Kennedy Stadium during an old-timers' game.

In 1987, Appling was still listed as batting coach for the Atlanta Braves.

MANAGING FOR ONE DAY

THERE HAD BEEN ECCENTRIC team owners before, but when the flamboyant advertising billboard and television tycoon, Robert Edward "Ted" Turner II, bought the Atlanta Braves in 1975, little did the world of baseball realize how strange the diamond game could become with a completely uninhibited owner running a major league franchise.

Turner was at his outrageous best during a special "Field Day" staged at Atlanta Stadium shortly after he took charge of the Braves when he got down on his hand and knees and pushed a baseball with his nose from third base to home plate.

Also in his earlier days as team owner he was often the star attraction at home game where his rooting from his private box became so boisterous that fans often paid their way into the park just to see Turner in action. In typical Turner fashion he would settle into his seat, doff his jacket, stuff a plug of chewing tobacco into his face, and bellow "Awwriight!" every time one of his players batted in a run or made an outstanding play in the field. Or after a foul ball sailed into the seats his celebrated frugal streak became activated as he sighed, "There goes four dollars," and, after three more fouls followed, he groaned "Sixteen dollars!"

ONCE HIS BRAVES BECAME so deeply mired in the second division that Turner threatened to call up his entire Savannah farm team to replace all his Atlanta regulars.

Early in the 1977 season, Atlanta under manager Dave Bristol began floundering badly and on May 10 the situation reached a climax when the Braves lost their sixteenth straight game. Turner could stand it no longer, so he ordered Bristol to go off on a ten-day "scouting trip" and appointed himself manager. On May 11 tempestuous Ted donned a uniform, ensconced himself in the dugout between two of his most trusted coaches (Eddie Haas and Vic Correll), and formally took over the reins as Braves pilot.

His players cringed at the sight of Turner in uniform because they knew his knowledge of the game's techniques was severely limited. For example, in his first days as owner, as his deputies explained the rudiments of baseball to him, Turner blurted, "What the hell is a bunt?" Despite the cringing and grumbling of his players, Turner called the shots for the entire game—with the assistance of his coaches—but he could do no better than Bristol as the Braves proceeded to lose their seventeenth straight game (to Pittsburgh) 2-1.

Most of the nation's baseball fans laughed at this moment of comic relief and Turner felt himself ready to manage for a while longer. However, National League President Charles S. Feeney was not amused and advised Turner that he was in violation of Major League Rule 20 which states in part: "No manager or player on a club shall directly or indirectly own stock or have any financial interest in the club by which he is employed except under an agreement approved by the commissioner. . ."

Commissioner Bowie Kuhn refused to give such approval and Ted Turner's managerial career ended after a single game in the dugout.

In that 1977 season Atlanta finished dead last in the National League's West Division with a dismal 61-101 record, but Ted Turner was still officially listed in all the standard baseball record books as being manager for a day with an 0-1 record.

◆

GO DOWN SWINGING

WALTER "SMOKEY" ALSTON, who managed the Brooklyn-Los Angeles Dodgers for twenty-three years (1954-76), winning 2,040 regular season games, came to bat only one solitary time as a big leaguer. Called up from Huntington, West Virginia of the Middle Atlantic league by the St. Louis Cardinals for the proverbial "cup-of-coffee" in September, 1936, he got into a game against the Chicago Cubs when regular first baseman Johnny Mize was ejected in the eighth inning for arguing with the umpire.

Alston, a powerful right-handed slugger who had belted thirty-five homers for Huntington, faced the Cubs star right-hander, Lon Warneke, took three hard swings and struck out. We must hasten to add, however, that Alston's middle strike was a vicious foul liner down the left-field line. In the field in the ninth, Alston cleanly handled one change, but booted a grounder, and wound up with a lifetime fielding average in the major of .500.

Alston continued playing in the minors through the mid-1940s, but Branch Rickey, wise old general manager of the Brooklyn Dodgers, recognized his potential as a manager early on and assigned him to pilot various Dodger farm clubs, including Nashua, St. Paul and Montreal.

FINALLY, IN 1954, Alston was called up to the major leagues for the second time, but this time as a manager he stuck. In 1955, he led the Dodgers to their only World Championship in Brooklyn and to a pennant in 1956 before the team moved to the West Coast. In Los Angeles his clubs captured world titles in 1959, 1963, and 1965 and pennants in 1966 and 1974.

In 1983, Walter Alton became the tenth manager to gain election to baseball's Hall of Fame at Cooperstown.

FROM BOSWELL TO BASEBALL

A. BARTLETT GIAMATTI, former president of Yale University and president of the National League since January 1, 1987, has brought a touch of class to baseball—he is the first authentic academician to hold a high administrative post in baseball's hierarchy.

Born in Boston on April 4, 1938, Giamatti developed a passion for baseball as a youngster and dreamed of some day becoming a member of the Boston Red Sox. Above all, he wanted to emulate his favorite Bosox player, Bobby Doerr.

His true talent, however, lay in the groves of academe, and in 1960 he graduated with a B.A. *magna cum laude* from Yale University. He continued on at Yale's Graduate School, winning his Ph.D. in comparative literature in 1964, after submitting a doctoral dissertation entitled *The Earthly Paradise in the Renaissance Epic*. Along the way Giamatti also studied under Yale's Professor F. A. Pottle, the renowned authority on the work of James Boswell, the biographer of lexicographer Samuel Johnson.

Giamatti taught at Princeton for a year and then returned to Yale in 1965 as an assistant professor of English and Comparative Literature. Giamatti almost immediately became a shining star on the Yale faculty and published a number of scholarly books, including: *Plays of Double Senses: Spenser's Faerie Queene* (1975), *The University and the Public Interest* (1981) and *Exile and Change in Renaissance Literature* (1984).

In 1978, at the age of forty, he was chosen as president of Yale University, becoming one of the youngest major university chief executives in the United States. Giamatti, however, was still a Boston Red Sox fan at heart and remarked just before his formal inauguration, "I'd much rather be President of the American League."

During his days as Yale prexy, Giamatti was often seen walking along the campus wearing rumpled slacks, a sports jacket, and a Boston Red Sox cap to go along with a beard labeled by *Newsweek* as "slightly satanic."

After little more than eight years at Yale's helm, Giamatti resigned his high academic post upon being elected president of the National League. Though he would have preferred the A.L., Giamatti reasoned: "Baseball beckoned, and a major league is a major league."

A league president is faced with myriad administrative tasks, many of them very difficult, and in this connection we interviewed Giamatti just prior to the July 14 major league All-Star Game played at Oakland's Alameda County Coliseum. In commenting about his N.L. duties in general Giamatti said:

"Determining legalities and illegalities in player contracts can be an extremely complex task. I can recall Yale professors translating cuneiform writing on Babylonian clay tablets in the Sterling Library dating back four-thousand years. I won't say that multipage player contracts are as difficult to comprehend as cuneiform, but some come awfully close. I've also spent a lot of time reviewing the ins and outs of the balk rule. People keep asking me why National League umpires are calling so many balks this year, and in response I just tell them that the pitchers are committing more balks. Period."

AT AN ALL-STAR GAME PRESS CONFERENCE at Oakland, Giamatti exhibited his sharp wit when a California sportswriter asked him: "Because there are so many home runs being hit in 1987, do you think the baseballs have been juiced up?"

"The baseballs are not juiced up any more than I am," retorted Giamatti. He went on to say:

"Naturally, I'm concerned with the baseball quality question because I've got my signature on every ball used in the National League."

In a study conducted by both major leagues, it was determined that the baseballs used in 1987 were no livelier than those put into play in previous years.

◆

ON AND OFF THE FIELD

7

PAYING FOR NOTHING

TOTAL ATTENDANCE FOR THE 1948 World Series, which pitted the Cleveland Indians against the Boston Braves, amounted to a very lofty 358,362, still the greatest crowds on record for a six-game Series. The Indians whipped the Braves, four games to two.

The record was set primarily because Cleveland's cavernous Municipal Stadium has a seating capacity of 78,000 (the largest in baseball), and Games 3, 4, and 5 were played at Cleveland, drawing a combined paid attendance of 238,491.

For Game 5, played on Sunday, October 10, the total paid crowd came to a whopping 86,288, the biggest turnout for *any* major league game up to that point. When all the seats were filled up, there were some eight-thousand people left over, who became standees and had to be accommodated behind the outfield fence.

More than five-hundred ushers and some five-hundred policemen were required to handle the crowd. (There were actually at least ninety-thousand persons in Cleveland Stadium that day if all the workers were counted, including ticket takers, refreshment stand workers, vendors, ground crew members, et al.)

Most amazing of all was that a sizable percentage of those eight-thousand standees could not even see the game! They had no chance, because it was impossible to see through people packed close to a fence. But, did they complain? Typical was one fan who paid $5 for a standee ticket (a lot of money for a sports admission in those days) who said: "I don't care whether I see the game or not....I brought my portable radio with me and listened to the game play-by-play, but I just wanted to be a part of the scene and hear the roar of the crowd."

Apparently most of those eight-thousand standees—enough to make up half an army division—felt the same way.

Nor did it seem to matter much that the Braves hammered the Indians that day, burying them by an 11-5 count as Boston third baseman Bob Elliott led the attack with two homers and four RBIs.

"Tomorrow's another day," said one of the Indians' loyal rooters. And so it was. On the next day at Boston, the Indians edged the Braves 4-3 behind the pitching of Bob Lemon to take the World Championship.

There had been many standing-room-only crowds at Cleveland Stadium in 1948 as the Indians set an all-time annual attendance record of 2,620,627 that stood for many years. The ballpark was the place to be—and to be seen—that glorious year in Cleveland, and if you had to stand for two or three hours and not be able to see much of the game, it didn't matter! A Cleveland Stadium filled to overcapacity for a ballgame was one of the grandest sights in all of baseball.

◆

UNIMPRESSIVE PRINTOUTS

DAVEY JOHNSON, as a clutch-hitting, smooth-fielding second baseman, acted as one of the spark plugs that helped Manager Earl Weaver make the Baltimore Orioles into one of baseball's top teams of the late 1960s and early 1970. Under Weaver, Johnson played on three straight American League pennant winners (1969-71).

Davey had a definite academic bent, especially in the field of computer technology. He attended Texas A & M University, received a bachelor of science degree in mathematics from Trinity University, San Antonio, and took a series of computer courses at Johns Hopkins University, Baltimore, during the off-season.

Weaver, on the other hand, was almost strictly a baseball man.

He began playing professionally as a seventeen-year-old straight out of high school, worked during the off-season as a hod carrier, and began managing in the minors by the time he was in his mid-twenties.

During the course of the 1972 season when the Orioles were floundering a bit (they wound up the year in third place), Johnson prepared an elaborate series of computer printouts that analyzed the strengths and weaknesses of opposing pitchers and batters. The twenty-nine-year-old infielder strongly believed that these computer analyses would help Weaver in developing strategies against all American League teams, especially against the contenders—the Oakland Athletics, Detroit Tigers, and New York Yankees.

As Johnson proudly strode into Weaver's office, he announced with obvious enthusiasm in his voice, "Skip, I really think the info in these computer printouts will give us an edge in every game we play.

Weaver, hardly looking up, grabbed the printouts, grumped out an unintelligible remark, and as soon as Johnson left the office, threw the whole batch of stuff straight into the trash can. "What the hell do I need all this mumbo jumbo for?" huffed Weaver.

As manager of the New York Mets since 1984, Johnson has won two pennants and one World Series title (he's never finished below second place)—and in the process he has utilized computer analyses liberally.

Toward the late 1970s, Earl Weaver himself is said to have begun to utilize computer-generated intelligence. "Well, I guess you've got to keep up with the modern malarkey to stay alive," Weaver reluctantly admitted.

◆

PAIGE AFTER PAIGE OF HUMOR

SATCHEL PAIGE IS ONE OF THE most colorful men ever to have played the game. He tossed out funny quotes with the same ease as he threw his scorching fastball or the pitch he called his "bee" ball (because when he fired it, it would be where he wanted it to be).

Paige was a star for an eon in the Negro Leagues. Due to the color barrier, he didn't get a chance to play in the major leagues until he was quite old. How old, exactly, nobody knew. Legend has it his birth certificate was lost, and Paige himself never knew his correct age. The generally held belief is that when Bill Veeck signed him to a big-league contract with the Cleveland Indians, Paige was in his forties. That made him the oldest "rookie" in the history of the game.

As a joke, Veeck even had a rocking chair placed in the bullpen for Paige's use. At any rate, "Satch" was often asked to philosophize on the subject of age. His most famous words, of course, were, "Don't look back. Something might be gaining on you."

But Paige, who once pitched a major-league game for the Kansas City Athletics as a special stunt, at the age of fifty-nine years, two months, and eighteen days (a record) also gave the world, "Age is a question of mind over matter. If you don't mind, it doesn't matter." He put another slant on the topic once by pondering in Yogi Berra fashion, "How old would you be if you didn't know how old you was?"

◆

LANGUAGE BARRIERS

LOU PINIELLA WAS an American League outfielder for many years. He was mainly known for his sweet swing and seething temper. As manager of the Mariners, Piniella recalled an argument he once had with Armando Rodriguez, an umpire who, like Piniella, spoke Spanish. Apparently the verbal exchange didn't last too long, "I cussed him out in Spanish," said Piniella, "and he threw me out in English."

Language barriers can be a real problem. Fresco Thompson, a famous Brooklyn dodgers scout, once told the sad tale of a French-Canadian minor-league prospect who couldn't hit a lick. "He's thinking in French, and they're pitching him in English."

◆

A PROLIFIC SPORTSWRITER

GRANTLAND RICE (1880-1954) by his own count wrote at least seventy-four million published words during his fifty-three-year career as a sportswriter. In his autobiography, *The Tumult and the Shouting*, Rice says he counted in this staggering output stories and articles he wrote for newspapers, magazines, and books. Thus, we can calculate that he turned out nearly 1.5 million published words per year, or nearly thirty-thousand every week for more than a half-century.

According to David Quentin Voight, one of the country's foremost baseball historians, Rice added new dimensions to sportswriting, especially in regard to coverage of baseball and football. Voight said: "We must remember above all that Grantland Rice was an unabashed romantic who rhapsodized over player-heroes and epochal games."

FANATIC FANS

WHEN BALTIMORE ORIOLES third baseman Brooks Robinson was inducted into baseball's Hall of Fame at Cooperstown, New York, in the summer of 1983, forty large buses loaded down with more than two-thousand of Brooksie's fans chugged in from Baltimore for the ceremony. Never before in history had a single inductee attracted that many fans to the Hall itself. Oddly, Robinson has never attended an induction ceremony since that time, although all Hall of Famers are strongly encouraged to come to Cooperstown for that gala occasion (all expenses paid, of course).

◆

MANGLER OF THE KING'S ENGLISH

ONCE DIZZY DEAN finally realized he was through as a pitcher early in the 1941 season (he pitched one inning for the Cubs in a game in mid-May and was tagged for three hits and three runs), he contemplated his future, and decided he wanted to become a baseball broadcaster.

The Falstaff Brewing Company, sponsors of the St. Louis Cardinals radio broadcasts, liked the idea of Dean's coming back to the Mound City, where he still ranked as a monumental heroic figure, and signed him to a contract to do play-by-play.

In his first appearance before a microphone early in June, Dean announced to his listeners, "I hope I'm as good a sports announcer as I was a pitcher," and then went on to charm his listeners with his peculiar brand of English. Runners "slud" into bases, pitchers "throwed" the ball, batters "swang," a hitter could look "mighty hitterish," or "stand confidentially" at the plate. Faking a double steal, two players "are now returning to their respectable bases."

Once he said "slid" correctly by mistake and he immediately "corrected" himself.

Radio listeners loved Dizzy's announcing, and the more he mangled the King's English the better they liked it. In 1942 Dean was judged by radio critics as "baseball's announcer with the worst diction," and in 1944, when he was doing both the Browns and Cardinals games, *The Sporting News* named Diz as "Announcer of the Year," and without any qualifiers.

He certainly didn't win any awards for objectivity, however, as he favored the Cards in particular. One day he roared into the microphone, "Well, here's Enos Slaughter, my ol' pal, walkin' up to the plate....Come on now, Enos, knock the ball down this guy's throat."

Dean committed his worst verbal atrocities in mispronouncing players' names: Stan Musial was "Moo-zell," Chico Carasquel "that hitter with the three K's in his name." Tony Giuliani was rechristened "Juli-Annie," but Dean was at his most outrageous when he wrestled with himself trying to pronounce the name of Cubs pitcher Ed Hanyzewski. "I like to have broken my jaw tryin' to pronounce that one," he said, with a trace of desperation in his voice, "but I said his name by just holdin' my nose and sneezin'."

Diz, who hated paperwork of any kind, never kept a scorecard or the batting "averuges." In this regard, he said, "I hate statics (statistics)…what I got to know I keep in my haid."

Dean's verbal miscues kept piling up with regularity, and as Curt Smith, a baseball broadcasting historian, said, "Each game with Dizzy Dean at the microphone assumed the air of a fresh performance, choreographed by the Ozark encyclopedist."

According to Diz, this batter had an "unorsodock stance," give that shortstop "a sist," a play made adroitly was "non-challoted," and a one-handed catch was "à la carte." When Cleveland loaded the bases, "That loads the Injuns full o' bases," and "a manager argying with an umparr is like argyin' with a stump....maybe you city folks don't know what a stump is. Wal, it's somethin' a tree has been cut down off of."

When the pace of a game slowed down, he often broke out into song, with his favorite number being "The Wabash Cannon Ball." He sang a bit off-key, by the way.

While Dean continued to be a big favorite among baseball fans throughout Missouri and points beyond, he did have his critics, and sharp ones at that. When the baseball commissioner, Kenesaw Mountain Landis, removed him from the network radio team for the all-St. Louis 1944 World Series, dubbing his diction "unfit for a national broadcaster," Diz, his feelings hurt, replied: "How can that commissar say I ain't eligible to broadcast? I ain't never met anybody that didn't know what ain't means."

I N THE SUMMER OF 1946, the English Teachers Association of Missouri termed Diz "a cultural illiterate" and demanded his removal from the air. In a formal complaint field with the Federal Communications Commission, the schoolteachers stated that Dean's broadcasts were "replete with errors in grammar and syntax" and were having "a bad effect on the pupils."

But in the spirited public debate that followed, powerful voices were raised to champion Dizzy Dean, including the *St. Louis Globe Democrat*, whose editorials attacked the teachers' "smugness."

Norman Cousins, editor or the prestigious *Saturday Review of Literature*, also rushed to Dean's defense as he extended his personal approval to Diz' linguistic style. Cousins emphasized that Dean was an individualist, both as a ballplayer and as a broadcaster, called him "an American original," and advised the critics not to tamper with the great man's unique style that had gained such wide popularity.

Dean was allowed to keep his job, but he did promise to clean up his act, at least just a little bit. In a touching statement when the case was being closed, Diz said: "I see where some of those teachers is sayin' I'm butcherin' up the language a little. Just remember . . .when me and Paul was pickin' cotton in Arkansas, we didn't have no chance to go to school much. All I've got to say is that I'm real happy them kids is gettin' a chance today."

Dizzy Dean went on despite the criticism to enjoy a long and extremely successful career in baseball broadcasting, a career that stretched on for some thirty-odd years in all, almost until the time of his death on July 17, 1973. He was invited to come to New York in 1950 to team up with Mel Allen in doing Yankee games. Then, beginning in 1955, he did the CBS television show *Game of the Week* for many seasons, and over a period of years worked on radio and television for other networks as well.

Commissioner Landis said earlier, as we pointed out, that Dean was not fit for national broadcasting, but an array of network executives thought otherwise.

Mel Allen recalled the antics of his old broadcasting partner: "Diz could get serious when you were talking, but once he took off solo, doing what passed for play-by-play, it was showbiz time. Missing a pitch or two, that never fazed him, and he was smart, intelligent, and you never knew when he'd break out into song.

"Dean had a method and style all his own. Nothing like it before…. Just look around. Nothing like it since. That's because you couldn't get away with the stuff he did then…they'd throw you out of the booth with the mike strangled around your neck."

Mel Allen, sports broadcasting veteran of more than fifty years experience, also indicated that many of Dean's mistakes in English were probably preplanned: "Diz always knew what he was doing. The things he came up with—a guy 'sludding' into third—they were professional. He knew sliding was the correct form, but he wanted to goof it up—it was a part of the vaudeville. But at the same time even more of his mistakes I'm sure were natural—they guy just didn't have much of an education. And he had an excitement about him."

One author of this book remembers when Dizzy Dean was doing the *Game of the Week* in the mid-1960s with Pee Wee Reese as his partner in the booth. By this time, Dean, never at a loss for words, had been behind the microphone for a quarter of a century and his style was definitely on the more polished side...not so many "sluds," "swangs" and "throweds" coming through at this point, but the grammar was still shaky and the speech colorful.

Asked one time if he was the greatest pitcher in baseball history, his replied: "Well, I don't know about that but I was right up there amongst 'em."

And among all the colorful and picturesque characters that came out of American baseball Jay Hanna "Dizzy" Dean was right up there with the likes of Casey Stengel and Babe Ruth.

◆

THE HUMAN SIGNING MACHINE

IN RECENT YEARS, Joe DiMaggio has been one of the popular attractions on the baseball "card show" circuit. Briefly defined, a card show is a baseball memorabilia convention where a variety of dealers offer their wares and where baseball stars—past and present—show up at specified times for autograph sessions. Run-of-the-mill players charge $4 or so per autograph. (Fans have to bring their own materials to be signed: autograph books, photos, baseballs, bats, etc.)

DiMaggio, voted "baseball's greatest living ex-player" ("At my age, I'm glad to be a living ex-anything"), had the highest going autograph rate, $15 a crack.

Joe played a starring role at the "Cincinnati Classic Baseball Card, Memorabilia, and Collectibles" show staged to coincide with the All-Star Game played on the second Tuesday of July 1988 at Cincinnati's Riverfront Stadium. During the course of two four-plus-hour sessions, Joe D signed two-thousand times! Veteran major league scout Ed Liberatore, a longtime friend of DiMaggio's, commented on these marathon autograph sessions: "That Joe DiMaggio is a human signing machine. No matter how many autographs he does in a day, his signature is always strong and bold."

Show promoters place a ten-signature per person limit, but there were still a number of staunch DiMaggio fans who were willing to fork over $15 each for 10 autographs. And no checks or credit cards, please. Just good old-fashioned cash!

There had been numerous complaints from baseball autograph addicts around the country that DiMaggio was charging a bit much for his moniker. In fact, the term "Yankee Clipper" started to be used in derision. What was Joe D's answer to all this criticism? Why, he simply raised the price to $18.

◆

EITHER OR

"DO YOU EVER GET WRITER'S CRAMP?" we asked Duke Snider at a recent baseball "card show" staged in New York City. Snider, who was appearing at two five-hour sessions, and signing an estimated two-thousand autographs, answered our question without a moment's hesitation:

"Well, I'd much rather sign a thousand baseballs than face Juan Marichal once. Marichal was absolutely the toughest pitcher I ever faced."

Marichal, who spent most of his sixteen-year big league career, 1960-75, with the San Francisco Giants, piled up a 243-142 lifetime record with a skinny 2.89 ERA.

"And I'd much rather sign autographs at $7 or $8 a crack than carry mail out of the Brooklyn Post Office at $3 or $4 an hour as I did in the off-season during my early years with the Dodgers in the late '40s and early '50s," Snider added.

He went on to say: "Baseball salaries—even for top players—weren't all that high a generation ago, and the chances for making extra money for personal appearances and that sort of thing were practically nil for most of my active career."

Nowadays Snider is obviously making up for lost time. When his autobiography, *The Duke of Flatbush,* came out in the early summer of 1988, his publisher scheduled an appearance for him at a midtown Manhattan bookshop. The lines of people waiting to buy copies of the Duke's autographed book stretched around the entire block!

◆

THE ALMOST DEADLY TARPAULIN

BACK IN THE OLD DAYS, tarpaulins were spread out to cover baseball fields overnight and then rolled back manually by groundskeepers, but now electrically operated tarps have come into vogue. Push a button and it can be spread over the infield in a jiffy—push another button and it can be rolled back just as quickly.

One of the classiest of all powered retractable tarps is operated at St. Louis's Busch Stadium, and by sheer accident it became a cause célèbre during the 1985 League Championship Series played between the Cardinals and Los Angeles Dodgers. Vince Coleman, the Cards' star outfielder and base stealing king, happened to be standing on the tarp along the first base side, casually warming up before the series fifth game, when a ground-crew member, not realizing anyone was still on the tarp, activated the rollup button. Within a second or two Coleman found himself trapped inside, being swallowed up as if a giant boa constrictor had wrapped its coils around him.

Coleman's screams brought out a rescue team, but not before some damage was done. His legs were so badly bruised that he could neither play in the fifth game, nor in the ensuing World Series that saw the Cardinals matched against the Kansas City Royals.

"The Coleman-tarpaulin episode certainly ranks as one of the strangest on-field accidents in baseball history," a St. Louis sportswriter commented.

"That tarp was a real man-eater," Coleman himself commented.

SOMETIMES WHEN BUSCH STADIUM is very quiet, one seems to hear faint murmurings from deep inside the tarpaulin machine, below the green artificial turf near first base.

"Vince," the machine seems to gurgle, like the crocodile seeking the rest of Captain Hook in *Peter Pan.* "Vince, come a little closer to me, Vince."

Coleman, sensing that the tarp machine's appetite was not yet satiated after it tried to ingest him, ran faster than ever—away from the "monster" machine.

◆

CROWNED BY BASKET OF TOMATOES

THROUGHOUT THE TUMULTUOUS 1940 American League season, the Cleveland Indians, Detroit Tigers, and New York Yankees were involved in a three-way dogfight for the pennant. The Yankees eliminated themselves in the campaign's final week by dropping a crucial game to the last place Philadelphia Athletics, while the Tigers, holding a two-game lead over the Indians, rode into Cleveland to play the final three games of the season.

Cleveland needed to win all three games, of course, in order to capture the flag.

Tensions always ran high between Detroit and Cleveland…for starters, the two teams formed a natural rivalry because of their geographical proximity, and over the run of the 1940 season a number of incidents exacerbated those tensions.

ONE OF THE WORST OF THOSE INCIDENTS occurred on a late Thursday afternoon, September 19, before the final series. The Cleveland Indians rolled into Detroit's main railroad station just a few hours before a scheduled night game with the Tigers.

Somehow about a thousand Tigers fans discovered the hour when the Indians would be arriving at the station, and like a well-trained military unit they formed a gauntlet at the gate through which the players had to pass. The Tigers fanatics greeted the tribesmen with "Cry Babies, Cry Babies!" catcalls. (The Indians had been dubbed "Cry Babies" because in mid-season they had unsuccessfully mutinied against their autocratic manager, Oscar Vitt.) But worse than that, the Detroit fans heaved tomatoes, eggs, baby bottles and assorted other objects at the Indians. It was the beginning of the "Vegetable War."

WHEN THE TIGERS WERE SET TO PLAY the Indians in the season-closing series beginning on Friday afternoon, September 27, the stage was set for a titanic clash. In an unusual pitching matchup, Bob Feller, the Indians ace with a 27-10 record, squared off against Floyd Giebell, a virtually unknown thirty-year-old rookie righthander, who had only pitched a handful of games in the majors. Tigers manager Del Baker threw Giebell into the game as a sacrificial lamb against Feller who was the odds-on favorite to capture his twenty-eighth victory. After all, Detroit needed only a single victory to take the pennant, and had to be stopped.

It was Ladies Day at Cleveland as some twenty-thousand screaming women jammed their way into Municipal Stadium with the total attendance very close to the fifty-thousand mark. In recalling that day years later, Bob Feller said:

"In that crowd were a great number of mysterious baskets and bags, carried by fans with revenge in their hearts. When Detroit's Hank Greenberg came up to take his swings in batting practice we got a sample of what was to come. A few tomatoes and eggs aimed at him came hurtling out of the upper deck. He grinned and waved at his tormentors.

"He didn't grin and wave in our half of the first inning, however. When Roy Weatherly, our center-fielder, lifted a high fly to left and he moved under it, the fans really cut loose with their ammunition. Greenberg was enveloped in a hail of vegetables, fruit, and eggs as he wandered around under Weatherly's fly. I still wonder how he caught the ball instead of an orange.

Left-field looked as though a big produce train had been wrecked in it. Umpire Bill Summers angrily ripped off his mask and called time. Then, as the barrage continued, he went to the public address system and threatened to forfeit the game. Manager Vitt also spoke over the microphone, pleading for a chance to win the ball game. The threat and the plea stopped the throwing as park police circulated in the stands.

It took the Indians' grounds crew more than a half-hour to clear the debris from the field. Hank Greenberg, who had regained his composure, helped out, grabbing one of the wheelbarrows to cart off a pile of vegetables and fruits. "Hammerin' Hank" was always known for his sense of humor.

When play resumed, the big crowd had pretty much simmered down as the police continued to scout the stands for potential violators. Toward the end of the second inning, however, they cornered a suspect in the upper left-field deck directly over the Tigers bullpen. As the police raced toward him the culprit dropped a heavy basket of tomatoes over the rail in order to rid himself of the evidence. Directly below, on a bullpen bench, unsuspecting catcher Birdie Tebbetts was hit squarely on the head by the basket and nearly knocked unconscious.

The police grabbed the perpetrator, a muscular twenty-five-year-old factory worker named Carmen Guerra, and escorted him down to a lower-deck security station. In the meantime, Tebbetts had recovered from the shock of the blow on the head and rushed to the area where the police were questioning Guerra. As the police held Guerra, an enraged Tebbetts allegedly punched the young man in the nose.

On the same day Guerra hired a lawyer and filed a $5,000 damage suit charging Tebbetts with assault and battery. Detroit club officials posted a $200 bond on the assault charge so that Tebbetts could leave town with the team. Later on, the suit was settled out of court.

In the fourth inning with the score 0-0, Feller walked Tigers second baseman Charlie Gehringer, and then Rudy York, the big first baseman, hit a curving lazy fly ball to left-field just along the line. Ben Chapman raced over and seemed certain to make the catch, but the ball dropped into the stands just beyond his outstretched hands and only a few inches inside the foul line. This home run, that traveled little more than 320 feet, turned out to be the blow that finally did in the Indians.

Feller allowed no further runs after that point and was touched for a total of only three hits, but the obscure Floyd Giebell pitched with the ease of a seasoned performer and shut out the Indians, scattering six hits. Final score: Detroit 2, Cleveland 0.

The Tigers staged a raucous pennant-clinching party that afternoon, but the Indians won the next two games to finish exactly one game out of first place, and just a single game ahead of the third-place Yankees.

As for Floyd Giebell, he never won another game in the major leagues. He made the Tigers roster as a relief pitcher in 1941, but he lacked control and was belted around so much that he was soon sent back to the minors and never resurfaced again into the majors.

That is strange baseball.

◆

SALARIES

DURING THE 1980S, baseball salaries reached a new summit with utility in-fielders given contracts caling for $500,000 or more per season. A generation earlier, although the dollar bought more, salaries were generally so low that unionizing became inevitable.

Take the case of Lou Boudreau, star shortstop of the Cleveland Indians, who as a sophomore in 1940 played in every one of the team's 155 games, batted .295, drove in 101 runs, and led American League shortstops with a .968 fielding percentage. For that effort Boudreau played under a contract calling for the munificent sum of $5,000—which amounted to little more than $30 per game (or $60 for a doubleheader).

Indians' owner, Alva Bradley, a business tycoon with interests in myriad industries, felt guilty about that contract, so he gave Boudreau a $2,000 bonus at the season's close. Then Bradley doubled Boudreau's 1941 salary to $10,000. Of course, there were no television revenues at the time.

Jeff Heath, the Indians outfielder from 1936 to 1945, continuously complained about having to play for "peanuts." After he hit .343 and drove in 112 runs in 1938, he was given a contract for the 1939 campaign calling for about $3,000. When he finished his major league career with the Boston Braves in 1949, Heath signed a contract with the Pacific Coast League's Seattle Rainiers in 1950 worth $25,000, the highest baseball salary he ever received.

When Jackie Robinson, the first black in the Big Leagues, was promoted from the Montreal Royals of the International League in 1947 to the Brooklyn Dodgers under Branch Rickey, general manager, he gave Robinson a $5,000 contract, the major league minimum at the time.

PLAYING WITH FIRECRACKERS

DURING HIS ELEVEN-YEAR tenure with the Cleveland Indians (1929-39), Earl Averill was a fun-loving, rollicking type of ballplayer who had the knack of keeping his teammates "loose" in the clubhouse and environs before a game. But one time he went too far with his merry ways and got himself into real trouble. While entertaining his fellow players with a mini-fireworks display in the home dugout at Cleveland's Municipal Stadium in 1935—around fourth of July time—his miscalculated the power of a fire-cracker and almost blew his right hand off. He was taken to the hospital and remained out of action for two weeks.

What got a little "loose" was the dugout.

◆

LOPSIDED BALLS

NOWADAYS THE MAJOR LEAGUE teams use a total of some four-hundred thousand baseballs during the course of the 162-game schedule, plus a couple of thousand more—at least—for the League Championships and World Series. If a ball shows the slight-est scuff mark from hitting a wall, or if it picks up too much dirt from being hit to the ground, it's supposed to be thrown out of the game immediately.

So it's easy to see why seventy-five or more balls can be used in a single game. Remember, too, that lots of balls are fouled off into the stands.

However, back during the so-called "dead-ball" days of the early 1900s, major league teams, along with the umpires, weren't nearly so free and easy in throwing bruised baseballs out of the game. Edd

Roush, whom we interviewed before the fiftieth anniversary All-Star Game played at Chicago on July 6, 1983, had this to say about the quality of baseballs used in the big leagues:

"Before the lively ball came into use after 1920, the only way you could hit a homer was if the outfielder tripped and fell down. The 'dead ball' just wasn't wrapped tight, and lots of times I caught them out in center-field when they were mashed on one side. Those lopsided balls still weren't thrown out of the game. Most of the time we'd use only four or five balls in a whole game."

Roush, whose big league career extended from 1913 to 1931, played mostly with the Cincinnati Reds and New York Giants. While with Cincinnati he won the National League batting crown in 1917 and 1919. Going into late 1987, Roush, at the age of 94, had the distinction of being the oldest living member of baseball's Hall of Fame.

◆

AUTOGRAPH HUNTERS

RUNNING THE GAUNTLET of autograph seekers can sometimes take its toll on a ballplayer. While many diamond stars try their best to accommodate fans, there are times when the clock says if you stop and sign, you'll pay a fine. In early August, 1987, New York Yankees outfielder Claudell Washington was running late for a night game in Kansas City. He tried valiantly to dodge the auto-graph seekers on his way into Royals Stadium and it cost him any-way. With a small army of clutching fans serving as an obstacle course, the trotting Washington tripped over someone's leg!

He was holding a briefcase in his left hand, and he tried using that hand to break the fall. The unhappy result was that Claudell scraped two fingers on his left hand so badly that he was unable to grip the bat properly and required more than a week on the bench before he could resume play.

The moral of this tale might be: If you're going to beat the autograph hounds, come to the park early or work on your end-around move.

◆

"STONE AGE"

SPARKLING FIELDING excites the crowd, and consistent field play results in great fielding averages.

Larry Bowa, National League shortstop for sixteen years (1970-85), mostly with the Philadelphia Phillies and the Chicago Cubs, and currently the manager of the San Diego Padres, set many National League fielding records. These include rolling up an amazing .991 fielding percentage for the Phillies in 1978, committing only six errors in 683 total chances. In 2,247 major league games, all but twenty-five as a shortstop (all the others were played at second base), Bowa made only 211 errors out of 10,198 total chances for a .980 percentage, another all-time shortstop fielding record.

Another record holder was Rich Dauer, Baltimore Orioles second baseman for a decade (1976-85), who committed only seventy-five errors in 5,013 total chances for a record .985 lifetime fielding percentage. Along the way, in 1978, Dauer set another record by going through eighty-six consecutive games and handling 425 chances without making a single blunder.

Noted as a glove man, Don Money, Milwaukee Brewers third baseman, committed only five errors in 472 total chances in 1974, good for a record .989 fielding percentage. In that same season, Money set another record by going through eighty-six straight games and handling 257 chances without a single miscue. In sixteen big league seasons with the Philadelphia Phillies and the Brewers (1968-83), Money, playing almost always at third base, made only 150 errors out of 6,089 chances, good for a lofty .975 fielding percentage. High fielding percentages at the "hot corner" are hard to come by.

By contrast infielders of an earlier era made errors by the gross. For example, William "Bad Bill" Dahlen, National League shortstop with Chicago, Brooklyn, New York and Boston from 1890 to 1913, committed the astounding total of 1,063 errors out of 14,294 total chances, resulting in a lowly .926 percentage. With Chicago in 1895, Dahlen led all National League shortstops in errors with eighty-four.

However, that's still not the one-season record for big league shortstops by a long shot, since Bill Shindle of Philadelphia in the Players League made exactly 115 errors in 1890. Nevertheless, no major league fielder at any position made more errors lifetime than did Dahlen. Incidentally, he wasn't called "Bad Bill" because of his fielding—he earned the nickname by being a dangerous clutch hitter.

Most errors at the keystone sack, 828, is the unenviable record set by Fred Pfeffer, National League second baseman with Troy, Chicago, New York, and Louisville for sixteen years from 1882 to 1897. And it took Pfeffer only 1,670 games to make that many boots—that's almost one error for every two games.

Hall-of-Famer John McGraw may well have established the record for the lowest lifetime fielding average at third base, .899. In a major league playing career that spanned 16 seasons, or parts of seasons, with Baltimore and New York from 1891 to 1906. "Mugsy"

McGraw miscued 394 times in 3,917 total chances. We must hasten to add that McGraw played a few games at second base now and then, but at any infield position he was a real "butterfingers." Good that McGraw earned his laurels as the Giants manager. We must also add that McGraw was not playing for also-rans—he was performing for championship teams.

Rattling off all these statistics does not necessarily mean that ballplayers or two and three generations ago were all that inferior as compared with today's denizens of the diamonds. Rather, the equipment used by the old-timers was clearly inferior, especially the fielders' gloves.

The old-time gloves, often dubbed "motormen's mitts," were small pieces of hard black leather that barely covered the hand. Many of them didn't even have fingers.

Today's gloves, on the other hand, are veritable miracles of the leather workers' art. The contemporary mitts are huge as compared with those used from the 1880s to the early part of the twentieth century, and they come with enormous webs to enable fielders to snag balls that would have entirely eluded the old-timers.

"The 'crabnets' they use today make fielding almost fumble-proof," observed Luke Appling who committed 672 errors while shortstopping for the Chicago white Sox from 1930 to 1950.

Moreover, groundskeeping has evolved almost as a fine art, with today's fields usually being kept in excellent shape. Some of the big league fields utilized during baseball's so-called "Stone Age" weren't kept much better than cow pastures, with bumps and hollows. Consequently, with a smooth field the ball has a much better chance of taking a "true bounce." And with artificial turf used in so many parks today, very few balls will take a bad bounce. They may bounce high unexpectedly, but generally stay straight unless they hit a seam in the indoor carpet, as happened in the 1987 World Series where the Twins faced the Cardinals.

Connie Mack, whose professional career as a player and manager stretched on for more than sixty-five years, from 1884 to 1950, once remarked that the error—the unexpected element in baseball—constitutes one of the most exciting plays in the game. "Take the error out of the game and baseball will be dead within a month," Mack stoutly maintained.

Well, judging by the bushels of errors committed in big league baseball fifty to one-hundred years ago, the game back then was certainly vibrantly alive and kicking.

◆

GUNFIRE

AL CICOTTE, who pitched for the New York Yankees, Cleveland Indians, St. Louis Cardinals, and Houston Astros from 1957 to 1962, recalled playing in the Cuban Winter League during turbulent days just at the time when Fidel Castro had come to power after overthrowing dictator Fulgencio Batista.

While he was pitching a game for Mariano against the Havana Sugar Kings at Havana Stadium on January 4, 1959, "there were tough-looking weatherbeaten soldiers from Castro's army all over the playing field, and two of them insisted on catching my warm-up pitches in the bullpen. The game started out quietly enough, but as I walked out to the mound to start the third inning, I heard a volley of rifle and machine-gun fire—approximately twelve to fifteen shots in all—from about two blocks' distance in the general direction of the center-field fence. While going through my motions on the pitching rubber, I immediately stopped everything I was doing as the entire crowd lapsed into a strange silence.

"We all waited for a few moments and, hearing no more shots, the umpire broke the silence by shouting 'Play Ball!' The game moved along without further incident into the sixth inning when I noticed groups of fans 'buzzing' everywhere in the stadium. The players in our dugout were told that several die-hard Batista army officers had had a running gunfight around third inning time with Castro's troops. The Batista officers were killed during the battle. After all this, our ball game didn't seem to be very important, although we were still battling for the Winter League pennant."

Cicotte, property of the Cleveland Indians at the time, left the Mariano team three weeks before the Winter League season ended. The Indians management insisted he come home because they didn't want one of their players to be exposed to stray hails of gunfire.

◆

BATTLING AGAINST BOOZE

BILLY SUNDAY'S main theme centered around "Battling with Booze." He deeply believed that hard liquor was the bane of all mankind, and if it were to be eliminated completely we'd all be well on the road to Utopia. Sunday traveled incessantly, especially throughout the Midwest and Eastern U.S. He toured many states, including Iowa, Illinois, Pennsylvania, and West Virginia in special trains, campaigning for temperance. During one of his campaigns in Johnstown, Pennsylvania, ten-thousand men in one meeting organized themselves into a "Billy Sunday Anti-Saloon League."

In Iowa, literally scores of towns and counties were reported as having "gone dry" as a direct result of the Billy Sunday meetings. Some thirteen or fifteen towns in Illinois visited by Sunday in a two-week period voted out the local saloon at Sunday's urging.

In a typical temperance speech filled with fire Billy Sunday would exhort: "The saloon is the sum of all villainies. It is worse than war or pestilence. It is the crime of crimes. It is the parent of crimes and the mother of sing. It is an appalling source of misery and crime in the land. And to license such an incarnate fiend of hell is the dirtiest, down-down, damnable business on top of this old earth. There is nothing to be compared with it."

And then Sunday hit at the nation's breweries by quoting from "De Brewer's Big Hosses," an 1880s temperance poem reading in part:

"Oh, de Brewer's big hosses, comin' down de road,
Totin' all around ole Lucifer's load;
Dey step so high, an' dey step so free,
But dem big hosses can't run over me . . ."

Through his fervent campaign against intoxicants of all types Billy Sunday became a major influence in the adoption of the Eighteenth Amendment to the constitution which prohibited the manufacture and sale of all liquors in the United States. The Prohibition Amendment went into force in 1920, and was not repealed until 1933. The "Noble Experiment" had failed. (Billy Sunday wouldn't appreciate TV baseball sponsorship by the breweries.)

Social historian Harvey Wish observed: "Both Dwight L. Moody and Billy Sunday ignored the basic economics and social abuses of the day except for their heated campaigns against the saloon. To the fundamentalist, Sabbath-breaking and drink were the chief social problems of the times."

BOBO NEWSOM DISDAINS PERFUME

LOUIS NORMAN "BOBO" NEWSOM, who pitched for eight major league and eight minor league teams from 1929 to 1953, was considered one of the roughest, toughest competitors ever to step on the pitcher's mound. At the height of his career with the pennant-winning Detroit Tigers in 1940, he was asked by a fragrance company to endorse a perfume.

Newsom, who was never averse to making an extra dollar, turned the offer down flat when he said: "Any fee I would receive wouldn't be worth the heckling I'd get from opposition dugouts."

◆

SHORTEST GAME

THE AVERAGE NINE-INNING major league game today requires about two hours and forty-five minutes to complete. However, a game can be played much faster as was proved by the Southern Association who conducted an experiment on September 19, 1910, to see just how fast. They proved that thirty-two minutes is all you really need.

In this 32-minute game, Mobile edged the home team Atlanta Crackers 2-1. With the score tied 1-1 in the first half of the ninth, Mobile pushed across the decisive run. Both teams hustled every minute of the way. Batters did not wait out the pitchers, but rather swung at every good pitch. There was only one walk; not a single player struck out; and Mobile even reeled off a triple play. Mobile made six hits against four for Atlanta. On the same afternoon, Chattanooga at Nashville in another Southern Association game, needed only forty-two minutes to complete.

STRANGE SPECIMENS

"BE CAREFUL HOW YOU HOLD THIS," Peter P. Clark, Baseball Hall of Fame Museum Registrar warned us as he handed over an artifact he pulled out of a cabinet in his lower-level museum office. We followed Clark's advice because this particular specimen of diamond-game memorabilia turned out to be a Gillette razor blade taped onto a sheet of letter paper inscribed with a note testifying to the fact that this blue blade was used by Cy Young on September 9, 1953, during a visit to a friend's house in East Cuyahoga Falls, Ohio.

The Cy Young razor blade is among numerous items in the Hall of Fame Museum collection not ordinarily placed on display. A razor blade in a baseball museum? Strange.

But that's not all. After Peter Clark gingerly placed the Cy Young Gillette blade back into the cabinet, he hauled out a chunk of wood, measuring about sixteen inches in length and some six inches thick. This solid-looking specimen of wood—more specifically red oak—was inscribed in pen as being the last block of wood cut with an axe by Cy Young, and dated November 8, 1954. Moreover, Cy Young, the 511-game winner, who spent his long retirement from baseball as a farmer in Newcomerstown, Ohio, autographed the chunk of oak soon after he chopped it. He was eighty-seven at the time. (Young died on November 4, 1955, at the age of eighty-eight.)

"The Cy Young oak is part of our permanent holdings, but one wonders what a collector would pay for it at public auction," mused Clark. "Almost any sort of artifact dealing with a Hall of Famer seems to have special appeal," he added.

Cy Young, the hard-throwing right-hander is, of course, baseball's all-time winningest pitcher with those 511 victories being rolled up over twenty-two seasons from 1890 to 1911.

ANOTHER HIGHLY UNUSUAL GIFT came to the Hall of Fame shortly after Johnny Mize was elected to baseball's shrine in 1981. The gift consisted of a large bucketful of red clay soil from the school playground in Demorest, Georgia, where Mize first began playing on the diamond. The contributor was Demorest's school superintendent.

In a fifteen-year major league career (1936-53, with three years out for military service in World War II), Johnny Mize slammed out 359 homers and averaged .312, while playing successively for the St. Louis Cards, New York Giants, and New York Yankees.

WHEN PHIL LINZ, New York Yankees infielder, played a loud harmonica in the back of the team bus after a late season 1964 game, manager Yogi Berra became so infuriated when Linz wouldn't "stop the music" that an altercation resulted. The "harmonica incident" led to Berra's departure as Yankees' pilot at season's end. Yes, Peter Clark has the harmonica—encased in its original box, no less—in his cabinet and it's been personally signed by Linz himself!

NELSON FOX ISN'T A Hall of Famer yet, but many baseball experts feel he should eventually gain election to baseball's shrine. During a nineteen-year big league career (1947-65), mostly with the Chicago White Sox, Fox batted a potent .288, lined out 2,663 base hits, and scintillated as a smooth fielding second baseman. After his premature death in 1975, members of Fox's family contributed a batch of the infielder's mementos to the Hall of Fame Museum. These included an unopened pouch of "Nelson Fox's Favorite chewing Tobacco." Fox was such an inveterate chewer that one of the major tobacco companies produced and marketed his own special brand of chaw.

A piece of terra cotta measuring about two inches across, about 1/2 inch thick, and shaped exactly like a tiny catcher's mitt, was sent to the Baseball Museum recently with an attached note reading: "This catcher's mitt was used by the wee people's baseball team in Ireland many centuries ago."

We don't know for sure whether or not the Irish leprechauns played baseball, but the tiny glove has been duly registered and numbered for exhibit purposes by Clark.

In regard to the leprechaun's "catcher's mitt," we should emphasize that one of the Hall of Fame's key exhibits, a worn, misshapen, homemade baseball had been discovered in 1934 in a dust-covered attic trunk in a farmhouse in fly Creek, New York, a crossroads village about three miles from Cooperstown. The farmhouse had been owned by Abner Graves, a boyhood friend of Abner Doubleday, who later claimed that Doubleday had "invented" baseball in Cooperstown in 1839. The ball, now known as the "Doubleday Baseball," was purchased for $5 shortly after it was found by Stephen C. Clark, a wealthy Cooperstown business-man, who founded the Baseball Hall of Fame and Museum in the late 1930.

It was an eighty-seven-year-old Abner Graves who convinced the Mills Commission of 1906-07 (the Mills Commission was formed by the two major leagues to probe the origins of baseball) that he was with Doubleday in 1839 when baseball had its birth. And when that ball, purportedly used in one of those early ball games at Cooperstown, was found at Fly Creek, the village's locale as the birthplace of the diamond game was further corroborated. However, these conclusions are still hotly disputed. Among other things, Abner Doubleday was a cadet at the U.S. Military Academy at West Point in 1939 and did not even set foot in Cooperstown at the time.

Nevertheless, without Stephen C. Clark, we would not have a National Baseball Hall of Fame and Museum as we know it today.

The so-called "Doubleday Baseball" is conspicuously displayed near the Hall of Fame Museum's main entrance.

◆

INDUCTING A DRYSDALE

IN THE HALL OF FAME'S first half-century of existence just over two-hundred players, managers, umpires, and executives were voted into baseball's shrine. A player must wait at least five years after his retirement from the game before he is eligible to be voted upon, and sometimes, unfortunately, a diamond star is elected to the Hall of Fame long after he's gone to the Great Beyond.

In the case of Don Drysdale, the right-handed power pitcher of the old Dodgers from Brooklyn had to endure a waiting period of fifteen years before he was elected to the Hall of Fame in 1984. Happily enough, he was very much alive and well when he finally received the call, but he almost missed out.

"Big D," as he was popularly known, posted a 109-166 won-lost record with the Brooklyn-Los Angeles Dodgers over a fourteen-year period (1956-69), and achieved one of baseball's truly note-worthy records in 1968 when he racked up six straight shutouts while hurling fifty-eight consecutive scoreless innings.

"Election into Baseball's Hall of Fame is the highest tribute an athlete can ever receive." That is not just the opinion of Edward W. Stack, Hall of Fame President, but of thousands of fans as well.

Hall of Fame Induction Ceremonies are always elaborately

staged gigantic media events with the newly minted enshrined being called upon to make speeches after receive the bronze plaques recording their deeds on the diamond. Thousand of fans from across the U.S.A. always jam their way into tiny Cooperstown, N.Y., when those Induction Ceremonies are held on midsummer Sunday afternoons.

Naturally enough, Don Drysdale, now a radio and television broadcaster with the Chicago White Sox, put together a carefully written speech to make at his induction. When his Chicago White Sox employers heard that "Big D" was planning to take the Sunday off, however, they were irked and told him straight out that his job status would be seriously jeopardized if he didn't show up for work in the broadcast booth that day as scheduled.

"It was touch-and-go for a while," said Drysdale. But after Drysdale made an emotional plea to his bosses pointing out that this was a one-in-a-lifetime thing (which, of course, they knew), and after a good bit more wrangling back and forth, he was finally given reluctant permission to travel to Cooperstown for his bid day! Strange?

◆

STRANGE SCHEDULING

FOR MANY YEARS the Pacific Coast League season consisted of two-hundred games or more involving many doubleheaders. The Oakland Oaks played one of the most unusual doubleheaders ever on April 13, 1913, when they met the Portland Beavers at home for a morning game. Then right after the game with the Beavers, the Oaks sailed across San Francisco Bay to play an afternoon tilt with the San Francisco Seals!

SUPER FAN

C. E. "PAT" OLSEN, a six-foot-two-inch right-handed power pitcher, signed a contract with the New York Yankees in 1923 as a twenty-year-old and was fully expected by the Yankees to become a star.

For the next five years Olsen labored in the minor league vineyards with stops at Des Moines, Pittsfield and Springfield, Massachusetts, St. Joseph, Missouri, Atlanta, and Amarillo, Texas.

"In 1924, I roomed with Lou Gehrig at the Yankees spring training complex at St. Petersburg, Florida, and thought I was ready at that time to make the big leagues, but I was sent back down to the minors just before the season began," Olsen said recently. "After my last stop with Amarillo of the Western League in 1927, I decided to call it quits as a ballplayer because by that time I knew I wouldn't make it to the majors...then I got into the oil business in Texas," Olsen added.

Over the years Olsen became an oil millionaire, but his passion for baseball continued unabated. In 1933 he attended the major league's first All-Star Game played at Chicago's Comiskey Park and from then through 1987 he never missed seeing any of the fifty-eight midsummer classics. He's attended nearly three-hundred World Series games from 1938 to 1987—in fact, from 1938 until 1980, Pat witnessed 255 consecutive World Series contests, missing the final game of the Kansas City-Philadelphia Series (at Philadelphia) because of a vital business commitment. That's the only Series game he failed to see in nearly fifty years. And he's gone to every Hall of Fame Induction Ceremony at Cooperstown since 1939.

"I doubt very much if any other fan has compiled an attendance record of this magnitude," observed Bob Fishel, Executive Vice President of the American League and a baseball executive with more than foty years of experience.

"I never made more than $300 a month as a minor league player, but once I established myself in business and had the time and resources to travel, I made up my mind not to miss a single one of baseball's premier events," said Pat Olsen.

♦

AN APPEAL TO AN AGENT

WHILE PLAYERS' AGENTS have reputations for being ruthless and greedy, they can also be reasoned with. For example, Lou Piniella, manager of the Seattle Mariners, tells a story about such an agent.

It seems one of the Mariners wasn't getting much playing time. Obviously the player's agent wanted his man on the field where he would have a chance to produce impressive statistics and thus earn more money. It was also obvious, from Piniella's point of view, that he couldn't play someone who was not performing well at the time. So when Piniella was faced with the rather irate agent who was demanding more playing time, the skipper had to be clever and somewhat diplomatic.

Piniella said, "I'd ask him, 'Do you like your job?'" The agent was no doubt quite puzzled at this seemingly evasive opening gambit, but replied, "Yes."

At that point Piniella came back with, "Well, I like my job, too, and I'm not going to keep it long if I keep playing your client." His tactic has worked more than once apparently, because Piniella concluded his tale by saying, "I don't get many calls from agents any more."

◆

POOR CHOICE OF WORDS

THE MINNESOTA TWINS began the 1996 season by undertaking a bold experiment. In Rick Aguilera, they possessed one of the best relief pitchers in all of baseball, a highly valuable commodity. They decided to try converting him into a starting pitcher, instead of continuing his normal role of being their "closer."

After working the first three innings of an early spring training game, Aguilera made his way to the clubhouse. As the game's starter, he had got in some light work and was through for the day.

He quickly showered and was ready to leave the ballpark even though the game was still in progress. Since he had usually worked the last inning of many of the Twins contests, it felt odd to be dressed and ready to depart while being in an empty locker room.

He commented later of that peculiar sensation by saying, "I hope I don't shower alone many times during the season."

Now, while a baseball fan knew what Aguilera meant, it was also clear that the quote sounded a bit odd, to say the least.

◆

NO SECURITY

PRIOR TO CAPTURING the 1996 World Series as the manager of the New York Yankees, Joe Torre had to realize his job was not exactly secure. First of all, his boss and Yankee owner, George Steinbrenner, has a reputation for firing managers with the frequency of most people changing their underwear. Secondly, no manager ever totally enjoys job security.

With all that in mind, when Torre was asked (before his World Series success) for his views on a plan to move Yankee Stadium to Manhattan in the year 2002, he was wise enough to know that a manager couldn't plan too far ahead. He replied with a grim sense of humor, "To be honest, it's not really my concern. You're talking to a guy with a two-year contract." By the way, for now at least, both Torre and Yankee Stadium are still in the Bronx.

◆

INTERPRETATION

IN THE SPRING OF 1994, there was a great deal of talk about a rather unusual situation facing the Los Angeles Dodgers. They had a rookie pitcher named Chan Ho Park who was from Korea. Since he spoke no English, the big question was whether the pitching coach would be able to communicate with him while making a mound visit during a game. Since baseball officials had ruled Park's interpreter couldn't go along for the conference on the hill, this was a very real concern.

Upon hearing all of the fuss, Graig Nettles, always noted for his humor, came up with a great quip. "I don't know what all this concern about the interpreter is all about," he opined. "George Scott (former Red Sox player) played fifteen years and he never had an interpreter." Scott, hardly known for his oratory skills or his dazzling articulation, probably was the only one who didn't enjoy Nettles's wit.

◆

"POETRY"

OVER THE YEARS the words spoken by baseball players have been carefully preserved as if they were precious lines from the mind of a poet. Ironically, most baseball quotes aren't meant to be taken so seriously. Still, many of the quotes are worth hearing, especially, especially the ones that show some creativity and wit. Surprisingly, baseball's funny lines often are full of figurative and rich language.

Ron Luciano was a popular umpire—that in itself is unusual. The fact that he went on to write several books and become a television analyst after his umpiring days is revealing. Luciano loved a hearty laugh even more than making his flamboyant calls on the diamond. He injected his sense of humor into all facets of his life.

Later he became a television announcer, frequently covering games which were not being carried nationally. Thus his words spoken into a microphone would only get widespread attention if the nationally covered game were rained out. This seldom happened, making backup announcers feel their work wasn't gaining much recognition. It could truly be a bit frustrating.

Luciano colorfully summed it up saying, "Doing the television backup games is like doing a telethon for hiccups."

◆

FIGURATIVE LANGUAGE

BOBBY MURCER, an outfielder for many years, also came up with a clever simile of his own. He was a fine hitter, but he couldn't stand trying to hit knuckleballs. That pitch is so unpredictable, nobody knows which way the ball will dart. Men who are power hitters and who love a diet of fastballs detest the elusive knuckleball.

A reporter asked Murcer what went through his mind when he had to face master knuckleball artist Phil Nickro. Murcer thought for a moment before coming up with, "Trying to hit him is like trying to eat Jell-O with chopsticks."

That's not unlike the quote attributed to pitcher Curt Simmons regarding the prospect of having to pitch to the great home-run hitter Hank Aaron. "Throwing a fastball by Aaron," said the hurler, "is like trying to sneak the sun past a rooster."

◆

ABSURD

WHEN BRYAN HARVEY was pitching out of the California angels bullpen, he was asked to list his lifetime dream. Harvey was apparently taking the question seriously (something ballplayers don't always do with such questions) as he stated, "Stop all the killing in the world."

While that was a fine sentiment, it somehow didn't mesh with his hobbies. His favorite pastimes were hunting and fishing. Quite an odd paradox!

◆

KINER-ISMS

ONE MAN FAMOUS, or infamous, for having an absurd way with words was New York Mets announcer Ralph Kiner. Here are a few of his gems:

* "All of Steve Bedrosian's saves have come in relief."

* When Kevin McReynolds was enjoying a great year for the Mets, Kiner informed his audience that McReynolds owned, "record-setting records."

* Kiner once imposed his wisdom that, "Third base is a reactionary position."

* Instead of identifying his show's sponsor as Manufacturer's Hanover, Kinder muffed the line from his "script" and called it "Manufacturer's Hangover."

♦

MORE ABSURDITIES

THE PHRASE "PLAY ME OR TRADE ME" is an old baseball line. The player who mutters those words is a man who has been benched although he feels he should be playing. His ultimatum is blunt, implying he is certainly good enough to play elsewhere. It is a line reeking with self-confidence on the player's part.

Once, though, a marginal player named Chico Salmon confused his manager with this unique demand, "Bench me or keep me."

Then there was Dennis "Oil Can" Boyd, a pitcher who could rival anyone when it came to zany quotes. When he was with the Red Sox, there was a bomb threat made on a flight the team was about to take. A writer asked Boyd what he thought about the situation.

Boyd managed to come up with these cryptic observations: "I don't know anything about it. They keep me pretty much in the dark about these things. Even if it had blown up, I wouldn't have known anything about it."

◆

MORE FANS

SOMETIMES SPECTATORS let loose a stream of unpleasant words about players and/or a team's front office. However, at times baseball players and officials have had the last word.

For instance, big-league pitcher Bo Belinsky was disgusted with the infamous Philadelphia Phillies fans. According to Belinsky, those fans "would boo a funeral." It's been said they'd boo Santa Clause as well.

Los Angeles Dodger fans, on the other hand, have a different type of reputation. It has been said the fans will attend games in full force, but aren't too knowledgeable. They have also been accused of being guilty of paying more attention to scanning the throng to see what celebrities are in attendance than actually watching the game.

One Dodger official summed it up by saying, "In Los Angeles twenty-thousand people will show up at the park accidentally, just to see what the lights are about."

The New York Giants played in the Polo Grounds before their 1958 departure to San Francisco. In their final season in New York, they managed to win only sixty-nine games while dropping eighty-five decisions. The fans weren't exactly packing the park. Even the last home game ever prior to the exodus couldn't draw a substantial crowd.

A Giants public relations man by the name of Garry Schumacher had the foresight, though, to realize, "If all the people who will claim in the future that they were here today had actually turned out, we wouldn't have to be moving in the first place."

◆

HALL-OF-FAME HUMOR

SOME PLAYERS WHO SUFFER through a tough game will boil with anger for hours after the contest. Many veterans, who have experienced years of going through both the good and the bad, manage to forget their fury upon leaving the ballpark. Hall of Fame pitcher Bob Lemon explained why he didn't take his problems home with him after bad outings throughout his fifteen-year stint. "I left them in a bar on the way home," he offered.

Joe DiMaggio has had myriad honors bestowed upon him. Aside from being inducted into Cooperstown's Hall of Fame, one of his finest moments had to be when he had been named baseball's greatest living athlete in a 1981 ceremony. The Yankee Clipper, still looking lithe at the age of sixty-six, commented with a big smile, "At my age, I'm just happy to be named the greatest living anything."

◆

ODD SOURCE OF HUMOR

FOR SOME REASON, baseball has been the sport of choice for many intellectuals. Therefore, it isn't too surprising to hear astute words being issued from scholars concerning the game. Perhaps the most famous words along these lines came from Columbia University philosophy professor Jacques Barzun, who profoundly stated, "Whoever wants to know the heart and mind of America had better learn baseball, the rules and realities of the game."

What is surprising, though, is a quote coming from none other than Albert Einstein that displayed a sense of humor and an interest in baseball. It seems Einstein once met baseball catcher Moe Berg. Now, Berg was not a run-of-the-mill ballplayer. He spoke many languages and was truly a brilliant man. Impressed with Berg, the great scientist suggested he would teach mathematics to the ballplayer and Berg in turn would teach baseball to Einstein. Then Einstein added a sort of humble concession, "I'm sure you'd learn mathematics faster than I'd learn baseball."

◆

LONG-DISTANCE CALLING

WHEN MILWAUKEE BREWERS pitcher Steve Sparks was a rookie, he suffered one of the strangest (and, in a way, funniest) injuries ever. Believe it or not, he actually dislocated his shoulder while, for some reason, trying to tear a phone book in half.

The Brewers' trainer, John Adam, came up with the best line concerning this situation. With a straight face he said, "This is one of the freakiest injuries I've ever seen; and a bit annoying because I had to look up a telephone number later."

◆

NEVER MEETING ROGERS

S EVERAL DECADES AGO, a pundit simply stated, "Will Rogers never met Howard Cosell." While his quote was terse, the meaning was clear to anyone with knowledge of the old saying, "Will Rogers never met a man he didn't like."

Cosell, a famous sports commentator, was very brash, so the Rogers allusion struck home. While such humor is biting, it should be noted that much of baseball's humor is indeed dark and scalding. Sometimes, though, the humor is not quite that strong, but remains at least somewhat sharp.

Bill Veeck, for example, could shoot off a derogatory line at times which carried the impact of a brushback pitch. He addressed the subject of Walter O'Malley once with a quote similar to the Cosell insult. Veeck called O'Malley, "the only man I know Dale Carnegie would hit in the mouth." Needless to say, these two men stood 180 degrees apart with O'Malley being as conservative as Veeck was liberal.

◆

SADISTIC HUMOR

IN JUNE OF 1993, the Florida Marlins were about halfway into their inaugural season. Not only did the Marlins have a slew of rookies on the team, even their ground crew was rather inexperienced. While Joe Robbie Stadium was designed and intended for play by the NFL's Miami dolphins, the transformation of the facility into a baseball park was successful.

However, when a downpour hit the stadium in midsummer, a new problem became apparent. The crew frantically tried to spread the tarpaulin onto the field before the game would be flooded out. Their efforts were in vain as the wind and rain stymied the crew. The opposing manager that night was Dallas Green of the New York Mets, who pointed out that after about fifteen minutes of frustration, the situation, "just got to be a little comical."

Ozzie Smith later said this was one of the funnies things he ever witnessed on television. "That was truly an experience watching the manager, Rene Lachemann of the home team, actually coordinating the crew, getting them into position. He had to show them how to correctly put the tarp on the field because the wind was blowing underneath it and it was very tough. By the time they finally did get it down, it didn't do much good anyway because the field was soaking wet then," Smith said with a grin.

Indeed, the more it rained, the heavier the tarp became, and the more difficult the task became. Florida's Jeff Conine was in stitches as he related, "When those guys dumped the water off the tarp and starting running with it, and then it got hung up, it looked like about twenty-two rotator cuffs went out all at once." Leave it to a player to come up with such an image.

◆

GRUELING STATS

IT WAS ENOUGH TO MAKE even Brooklyn Dodgers' fans cringe. Their beloved team went through a grueling stretch back in 1920 that remains unmatched to this day. It began with a May 1, 1920, marathon. The Dodgers played in a twenty-six-inning affair which set a record for the longest game ever and ended in a frustrating 1-1 tie. Incredibly, the next day they engaged in a thirteen-inning contest, which was followed by a nineteen-inning grind on the third day. In addition to all that, their fifty-eight innings over that span were played at three different settings, creating quite a demanding trip!

◆

A MOVING EXPERIENCE

ON MAY 2, 1996, an earthquake rocked Seattle during a game between the Mariners and the Indians. The quake, which registered 5.4 on seismographs, shook the Kingdome for about fifteen seconds. Although nobody was hurt, chaos ruled for quite some time.

For example, the Mariners radio announcer Dave Niehaus told his listeners, "I think we're having an earthquake. I'm out of here!"

Meanwhile, on the field the two managers, Lou Piniella and Mike Hargrove, were conferring. Piniella asked Hargrove what he wanted to do. The Tribe skipper replied, "We've got two choices: finish the game, or I go back to our hotel and go up to my room on he thirty-fourth floor. What do you think I want to do?"

Well, the game was suspended, but even out of potential tragedy came more of baseball's unique humor. For example, the very next day, Seattle's Norm Charlton turned in a zany report. "When I got home (from the suspended game)," he began, "my clothes were strewn all over the place and the pictures were off the wall." He paused dramatically, and then added, "But that's the way it was when I left."

◆ ◆ ◆

INDEX